New Directions
in the Study of Language

ERIC H. LENNEBERG, *Editor*

New Directions
in the Study of Language

The M.I.T. Press
MASSACHUSETTS INSTITUTE OF TECHNOLOGY
CAMBRIDGE, MASSACHUSETTS

Second printing, first MIT Press paperback edition, August 1966
Third printing, August 1967
Fourth printing, September 1968
Fifth printing, October 1969
Sixth printing, September 1970
Seventh printing, May 1970

ISBN 0 262 12011 9 (hardcover)

ISBN 0 262 62005 7 (paperback)

Library of Congress Catalog Card Number: 64-8088
Printed in the United States of America

499 #

Preface

In the fall of 1962 I was asked to organize a symposium for the XVIIth International Congress of Psychology which was to meet in Washington in August 1963. It seemed to me that an international congress is not the place to report on specific research projects, nor a forum at which recent research is to be reviewed in the style of the various yearbooks or review volumes that are published annually. Instead, I intended to use this occasion to encourage the most outstanding scientists in the field to discuss the phenomenon of language in the light of their specialized knowledge, to encourage them to point to new and unsolved problems, to vent their enthusiasm, and to speculate freely. I was confident that interesting speakers, thus roaming over wide areas of knowledge, would enable us to attain a new synopsis and spark our intuition.

I was successful in securing the cooperation of all of my number one choices with two exceptions, Roger W. Brown and Susan Ervin, both of whom were already involved in another symposium at the same congress and were thus barred from participation in a second one. They were both planning to deliver papers on important aspects of language behavior, and I was fortunate in persuading them to allow me to include their congressional contributions in this volume. Professor A. R.

Luria from Moscow had also planned to attend the symposium and deliver a paper but at the last minute was prevented from coming because of ill health. Thus a lacuna was created in my original schedule of presentations which had to be filled at the eleventh hour. It was too late to solicit the help of any of the best known scientists, and so I boldly condensed some hitherto vague thoughts of my own into the paper that is included here. This is the reason for listing my own name among a cadre of scholars to whom I have unblushingly referred as my number one choices of speakers! The symposium had the title Language and the Science of Man; it was ably chaired by Professor R. Meili of Bern, and Dr. F. Goldman-Eisler agreed to serve as formal discussant.

Since there are two distinct origins of the following articles, namely, (1) the papers contributed to the Symposium on Language and the Science of Man and (2) papers contributed to other symposia of the International Congress, it is not surprising that the articles are of two distinct styles. The first four afford a wide-scope view of language problems, and each one makes an attempt to adumbrate these problems with broad implications for various fields of inquiry (maturation, social anthropology, human biology, and experimental psychology). The last two articles, however, are more specifically concerned with one important area in the psychology of language, primary acquisition of speech and language.

Dr. Goldman-Eisler's contribution to this volume falls into two divisions; first there is an edited version of her formal discussion of three of the symposium papers (she felt that Dr. Leach's paper on language in the light of social anthropology was outside of her competence); then there is an expanded version of material that she presented orally at the time of the meeting. From the brief remarks in the course of that discussion it was obvious that some highly original and stimulating work was being compressed into all too scanty postconference remarks which deserved to be dealt with in much greater detail. Therefore, I asked Dr. Goldman-Eisler to submit a regular article in addition to her formal discussion. Originally she had agreed to this; however, subsequent illness made it impossible for her to send in a full-fledged article in time for our publication deadline, and so we had to satisfy ourselves with a single contribution in two parts.

I have tried to explain the reason for the heterogeneity of the present collection. At first I was in doubt whether there was enough of a common denominator to warrant a joint publication. I decided in favor of it because, after seeing all the papers together, I felt that there was here an excellent cross section of language research at midcentury. The issues that concern us today are definitely different from those at the beginning of the century. New problems are recognized and new avenues towards possible solution are being suggested. This little volume aims at characterizing some of the important new trends.

I would like to thank the Harvard Educational Review for giving permission to reprint the article by Bellugi and Brown; S. Karger AG, Basel/New York for allowing me to reproduce the photograph of the bird-headed dwarf; and W. F. Brewer for supplying me with the pedigree shown in Figure 2 of my article.

E. H. L.

Contents

ix

LEONARD CARMICHAEL*

The Early Growth of Language Capacity in the Individual

The speech of man is one example of the many devices used by living organisms to influence the behavior of other living organisms. From a biological point of view, human speech involves specialized sense receptors, anatomical structures for the production of sound, and complex neuromuscular mechanisms to control, modulate, and direct the vibrations that are emitted.

The hearing and the behavioral response to speech thus involves specific sense organs and related neural and motor systems. On both the sensory and the behavioral sides these capacities that make speech possible have had a long history in the evolution of the animal series, and each human individual must pass through a series of developmental stages in achieving adult linguistic capacity. The present paper is primarily concerned with the very early development of speech mechanisms in the individual, but this growth can possi-

* National Geographic Society, Washington, D. C.

1

bly best be understood if it is first considered in a general evolutionary setting.

Students interested in the early beginnings of social communication in its most basic forms have investigated the ways in which bacteria, unicellular organisms, certain plants, colonial organisms, invertebrates, and vertebrates react to patterns of stimulation that originate in the activities or in the mere presence of other organisms.

In many cases, the interstimulation and response of such organisms may be seen by an external observer to involve what may be called the transmission from organism to organism of at first very simple, and later more and more complex, types of information. This information, transmitted by signals, may initially indicate the mere presence or absence of other individuals. Later this primitive form of communication may involve such matters as the direction of spatial movement in an almost tropistic way, determined in nearby individuals by the change in place of other individuals. As evolution progresses still further, more and more specialized and complicated units of information that are of biological significance in the life of individuals are transmitted from organism to organism. Stimuli arising from the nonliving environment often also affect and modify such social stimulation.

The classical work of K. von Frisch (1923) on the specialized motor activities of worker honeybees, by means of which new knowledge of the location of supplies of nectar or pollen can be transmitted to other members of the hive, may be taken as an example of social transmission of relatively complex information by social insects. Similarly, ants, termites, and many other forms of insects show examples of social interstimulation and response that are important to these organisms biologically and that involve what must be called "information communication." The very varied strident calls of certain insects have even led some writers to make unwarranted assumptions about so-called "insect speech" (Warden, Jenkins, and Warner, 1940).

Other senses than that of hearing play a role in insect communication. A female of a large moth such as the cecropia, placed in a window at night in a screened box, may, before morning has come, almost certainly by olfactory stimulation, have attracted one or more males of the same species. It is believed that the male moths may sometimes have had to fly a distance of as much as three miles in order to reach the female moth (Rau and Rau, 1929).

The production of high-frequency sounds as a means of determining the precise orienting behavior of bats, and the consequent capturing of insects in the dark by these mammals, is a well-known example of the biological use of high-frequency auditory stimulation in determining mammalian food-getting behavior. Recent work of Kenneth Roeder (1963) and his associates shows that certain forms of nocturnal moths are also capable of receiving these humanly inaudible high-frequency stimuli produced by hunting bats, and of responding so quickly in their flight that these big insects frequently avoid capture by their would-be predators.

The cases just cited are merely a few examples of

the innumerable ones that could be given to show the biological utility of various forms of signals used in the life patterns of animals below the vertebrates.

Inframammalian vertebrates also communicate with each other in many ways. Birds, for example, use a variety of sounds and motor displays to direct the behavior of individuals of the same or other species and of potential predators (Armstrong, 1947). Much the same may be said of many specific behavior acts of fish, reptiles, and amphibians. The recent work of members of the ethological school in their studies of animal behavior has led to a scientific description of many new examples of such forms of communication, often involving what may be called fixed or even inborn meanings, as related to very specific stimulus patterns such as the shapes of predators (Tinbergen, 1951).

Mynah birds and other infrahuman organisms can be taught to say words and even to repeat relatively long sentences. W. M. Mann (1930), who for many years directed the National Zoological Park of the Smithsonian Institution, trained a Mynah bird to say, "How about the appropriation?" These verbal sound patterns were made by the bird on a signal from Dr. Mann when he was entertaining the then Director of the Bureau of the Budget at the Zoo. Scientifically, who was communicating what with whom in this case deserves a few moments of thought.

This example of the Mynah bird's vocalization serves to illustrate the difference between true human speech and the mere organization of sounds that can be interpreted by human observers as those of speech. For Dr.

Mann and for the Director of the Bureau of the Budget, the pattern of sound produced by the Mynah bird was indeed "meaningful speech." Almost certainly this was not in the same sense true for the bird. It may be remembered in this context that blind persons have had secretaries or members of their families taught to read aloud languages such as Greek, which were unknown to the readers, without instructing the readers in the language. The blind person thus hears and understands the language that is read, even though the human sound producer is unaware of the significance of the sounds he is producing.

In infrahuman mammals, it is thus clear that the control of the behavior of individuals of the same species, as well as the behavior of other living organisms of different species, is accomplished by a variety of forms of motor activities which produce energy changes that serve as stimuli to the receptors of the other organisms. The receptors involved include those specialized to be acted upon by pressure and the stimuli for smell, taste, and sight, as well as by air vibrations with the physical dimensions of effective vocal stimuli.

Biologically speaking, therefore, the study of the onset and evolution of communication must not be limited to the capacity to produce what may be called "meaningful" words or to the capacity to hear utterances which the older writers on language used to speak of as "capable of transferring meaning from one individual to another." B. F. Skinner (1957) has recently given a most insightful consideration of the modern understanding of the word "meaning" as it is used in studies of verbal behavior. This consideration of "meaning" is not intended to imply, however, that effective normal adult human speech may not be used to control the behavior of other human or infrahuman organisms who do not fully "understand" such speech. The verbal control of the behavior of dogs, horses, and other animals by vocal signals, such as patterns of loudness or of pitch, are common examples of such forms of communication. Such sound signals have in one sense true "meaning" and may play an important role in the ongoing temporal context of the essential behavior of animals and men. Such vocalizations may be thought of as preliminary stages antecedent to true fully-developed human meaningful speech. It may be better, in order to avoid confusion, not to consider these patterns of meaningful sound signals as true speech. The use of words in this context is well illustrated in the report of R. M. and A. W. Yerkes (1935) on vocalizations. They say:

Among categories of social behavior none is more important than intercommunication. As we use it the term is inclusive of language. Speech, as applied to human systems of intercommunication, does not occur in any infrahuman primate. Language, however, in varying degrees of complexity and in diverse forms, is exhibited, and there are in effect languages of attitude, gesture, scent, sound and possibly still others not suggested by human experience and observation. Our experience in the study of monkeys and apes leads us to doubt whether, apart from representation of ideas, intercommunication is more serviceable in man than in certain other primates. In us speech is at once highly complex and incomparably serviceable, whereas in monkeys and apes other linguistic systems have been developed which possibly serve the needs of the organism even better than would spoken language. It would be difficult indeed to exaggerate the importance of intercommunicational symbols and systems in the social life and organization of primates from monkey to man.

The very recent and extensive work of Jane Goodall (1963), in her incomparably complete studies of chimpanzees in the wild, well shows how subtle and important is a most wide range of vocalizations in the organization of the complex everyday social life of these great apes.

On the basis of these observations on the role of communication in animals below man in the phylogenetic scale, we may now turn to the major topic of this paper, the early ontogeny of language in the young human individual. In the developing infant a sequential series of what may be called emergent stages of vocalization can be described both before and after birth. This development can be thought of most clearly in the light of the evolution of the forms of communication that have just been sketched in animals below man. The old idea of the biogenetic law or theory of recapitulation as an explanatory principle of human growth is thoroughly discredited, but it is not without interest to note that there is a certain parallelism between the growth of the capacity for various forms of communication in the animal series and in the ontogenetic development of each human individual. The neonate makes sounds which serve a biological purpose in the control of the behavior of attending adults well before human speech in its narrow and specialized sense develops.

In some babies, however, well before the end of the first year of postnatal life, real meaningful speech has begun. Various studies put the average time for this onset at eleven months with a range from about eight to twenty months as the time for the appearance of the first meaningful word (Bühler, 1954). No one who considers with care the sensory and behavioral developmental sequences in the growing human infant during its first months can fail to recognize the descriptive value of the concept of *emergence* in noting the steps that are always antecedent to the uttering of the first meaningful word by the individual. Each developmental stage of vocalization is in some respects unique in its characteristics, and no developmental level is ever a mere sum of previously described and pre-existing antecedent capacities or processes. Thus, a longitudinal study of the same human infant over a period of time such as the first two postnatal years best shows what combinations of capacities are the invariable antecedents of later and, in their turn, fully novel emergent vocal characteristics. Each such stage thus marks a step, as it were, in the progress from the mere emission of sound to true, meaningful human speech.

It thus becomes clear that one who wishes to trace the history of the growth of language in the individual should first consider, at least as an analogy, as has been done in this paper, something of the growth of communication in the animal series. On the basis of this knowledge it is helpful to start in the infant at some well identified stage and one by one go back and back and describe the capacities that are recorded as present in relevant, and essentially invariable, temporally antecedent stages (Carmichael, 1956).

In the study of the ontogeny of human speech, this

procedure of tracing back from surely meaningful to surely nonmeaningful sound production is not easy. There are great individual differences in early language development in normal and abnormal infants. Part of the difficulty in considering all of the early developmental stages in the prelinguistic utterances of infancy is also found in the failure of many students to agree upon the terms to use in describing the phenomena that are observed. Gaps in the sequence of development are often very puzzling, as Dorothea McCarthy (1954) points out in the following sentence:

There is a tremendous psychological gap which has to be bridged between the mere utterance of the phonetic form of a word and the symbolic or representational use of that word in an appropriate situation.

The dramatic emergence of meaningful speech has been discussed by G. A. De Laguna (1927) in an observation on the linguistic development of one of her own children. When about eight months old, her child learned to point to an object which attracted her attention. A clock was pointed out to the child and the words, "tick, tock," were enunciated by the adult. Soon the child, instead of pointing, whispered, "tee, tee." "Tee, tee," De Laguna emphasizes, however, was thus still far from being a name. It was still used indiscriminately as a means of pointing to a variety of objects. This "tee, tee" was, she says, "the announcement that something interesting is at hand and the summons to look at or attend to it." At length, however, the child under observation learned in pointing to the moon to substitute the words, "moon, moon." At first this response was used only when she was carried to the window and the moon was pointed out. Then one night the child was carried along a street lighted by large round lamps. In great excitement she pointed to one, repeating, "moon, moon." From this time on, the child rapidly acquired a true vocabulary of meaningful words. The similar dramatic learning of the word, "water," when Helen Keller's teacher, Anne Sullivan, held her hand under running water in the pump and at the same time spelled "water" into her hand by a tactual alphabet, is worth noting here (Keller, 1913).

To many students of language, the events that follow the development of the capacity to utter or respond to the first word in the "meaningful" way just indicated is the beginning of the consideration of true human speech. In the present paper, however, the effort will be made to trace backward the ontogeny of the stages that lie behind this first uttering of a meaningful word. The stages in the early development of the individual that will be noted may properly be considered as typical, and perhaps essential, antecedents to the production of the first word or words that carry the so-called true meaning of adult human speech.

Some of the principal research findings that determine the age, between birth and the use of the first meaningful word, at which specific emergent capacities appear, have been summarized in some 67 steps in an excellent table compiled by McCarthy (1954). This table shows the age at which selected vocal items are reported as present in a number of studies of the early linguistic development in infants. The studies on which this comprehensive table is based lead one back through a series of what must be considered emergent levels to the very first vocalizations of the newborn human infant and even back into fetal life. Until recently nearly everyone who has interested himself in the ontogeny of language and speech has begun his study with an account of the "birth cry." An article of interest to historians of philosophic thought could be written about the attitudes that have been expressed concerning the phenomenon of prenatal and immediately postnatal behavior. W. Preyer (1893), a great early German experimental student of child development, quotes the philosopher Kant as saying:

The outcry that is heard from a child scarcely born has not the tone of lamentation, but of indignation and of aroused wrath; not because anything gives him pain, but because something frets him; presumably because he wants to move, and feels his inability to do it as a fetter that deprives him of his freedom.

Preyer points out quite correctly the futility of such a fanciful interpretation of the birth cry. It is interesting that in more recent times some psychiatrists, particularly those who are interested in psychoanalysis, have seen special meaning in the cry of the human infant at birth. Blanton (1917), for example, has written of the cry:

It is an expression of its overwhelming sense of inferiority on thus suddenly being confronted by reality, without ever having had to deal with its problems.

Knowledge of the condition of the human cortex at the time of birth makes such statements especially surprising. A realistic and scientific study of the birth cry, of course, sees in it merely one stage in the development of the mechanisms that later will make meaningful vocalization possible.

The human vocal apparatus may be compared to a wind instrument in which the bellows are the lungs and in which the larynx and windpipe form a reedlike instrument. The pharynx, the mouth, and the nose provide resonating chambers. It is by no means proper to think that this wind instrument is in its final form at the end of the fetal period. At birth, for example, the vocal cords are shorter than in later life (Feldman, 1920). The alterations that take place in the so-called "change of voice" in the male during adolescence show for how long a period growth processes continue in the development of this instrument. The receptor organs involved in the social intercommunication of language in the individual also develop during prenatal life to the point at which the stimulus patterns related to sound and other types of signals can effectively activate and direct the behavior of the growing individual.

The birth cry, for all its dramatic place in the history of thought about the infant, is not even the first sound of which the human individual is capable. There are records in the medical literature, in cases of difficult birth, of *vagitus uterinus* or fetal crying. This phenomenon is observed when the sac is ruptured before birth and the baby begins to breathe air prior to delivery (Graham, 1919). Minkowski (1922) and others have noted crying in operatively removed fetuses of approximately 6 months postinsemination age. Some components of the mechanism that make crying possible are functional at even earlier fetal age. In operatively removed fetuses between 4 and 5 months of age the opening and closing of the mouth and rhythmic chest actions of the sort often named Ahfeld's breathing movements have been observed. Air breathing, which is all-important in the first production of true human sound itself, has been reported in human fetuses in "fits and starts" before the sixth month (Carmichael, 1954).

As just noted, speech in a biologically functional or social form depends not only on the production of air-borne patterns of vibrations, but also upon hearing. Many studies agree that at birth, of all the senses, hearing "slumbers the most deeply." There are a good many investigations which confirm the fact that the newborn baby does not hear at all, or at least hears poorly, sounds of ordinary intensity and vibration frequency. It has been asserted by those who have studied the neonate during its first hours that air breathing, yawning, and crying are typically required to open the Eustachian tube, and thus allow what is described as the gelatinous liquid of the middle ear to drain out before hearing is established (Carmichael, 1954). There is evidence, however, that the sensory receptors of the inner ear themselves are functional well before the time of normal birth. Responses to loud sounds in unborn fetuses have been reported. Electrophysiological techniques demonstrate the functional capacity of the auditory receptors in mammals during fetal life (Rawdon-Smith, Carmichael, and Wellman, 1938). Visual, touch, and muscle receptors, all of which play some part in fully established, adult interpersonal communication, are also all functional before birth (Carmichael, 1954).

In some detail the present writer has described what he has named the law of anticipatory morphological maturation (Carmichael, 1954). This law states that structures are frequently, indeed almost invariably, sufficiently mature anatomically to be activated experimentally at a temporal period in development before that at which they are required to play a useful or biologically adaptive role in the economy of the organism. This law is well illustrated in the development of the complex structure basic to the individual's ability to use speech.

Following the discussion given above of the meaning of the word "emergence," it seems obvious that the receptor mechanisms and the motor mechanisms of speech are functional at birth and even before birth. Some postnatal development of these mechanisms does take place, but, clearly, postnatal linguistic growth is largely dependent on the maturation of specific brain mechanisms. These are the brain centers that are known to be essential in adult speech.

The areas of the brain that are basic to speech are very complex and as yet not fully understood. In considering speech centers, Penfield and Rasmussen (1952) and many other students have emphasized as important a complex of functionally related areas. These include two bilateral cortical areas that seem basic to vocalization, the Rolandic and the superior frontal regions. These have been demonstrated to be important in the speech functions of adults. Besides these areas, there is evidence of the importance of three cortical areas in the dominant hemisphere in normal and abnormal speech. The first of these, properly named for its discoverer, Paul Broca, is found on one or two convolutions just anterior to the precentral gyrus and above the fissure of Sylvius. The so-called parietal speech area and an area in the posterior temporal cortex of the dominant hemisphere are also both known to be important in speech and especially in the aphasias.

The rate and character of the growth or maturation of different parts of the brain of any species including man, both before and after birth, it is agreed, are largely determined by heredity. In the human individual it is important also to remember that such differential maturation continues long after some changes in the response correctly attributable to individual learning can be demonstrated.

In analogy with a frequently used term descriptive of the time when the child can effectively be taught to read, that is, "reading readiness," it is clear that in the human individual the maturation of certain brain centers is necessary to produce a state of the brain that may be called *speech readiness*. It also seems likely that this readiness is not a characteristic of the total brain, but rather of quite specific brain mechanisms that play a role in making human speech possible. In other words, in the postnatal life of the infant certain centers of the brain of the growing infant must reach a specific level of development before the learning of linguistic patterns that are "meaningful" is possible. This level of brain capacity must emerge before the child begins to learn the linguistic forms that are typical of the social group in which it is being reared.

There is still much to be learned about the differential rate of development, during the months that follow birth, of the gross and fine anatomical structures of the brain areas basic to language. A review of the current literature on this subject suggests that this "late embryology" of the brain is still a surprisingly neglected area of scientific study. Some facts about this differential maturation, however, may be noted. It is believed that the number of brain cells does not increase after birth. Many different types of growth changes do, however, occur in brain-cell populations during the months and years of postnatal maturation. A number of different forms of developmental change during postnatal life have been studied in relation to a demonstrated increase in functional capacity. Among these alterations are the development of Nissl's bodies in the neurons, the growth of increasingly complex dendritic networks, and the selective rate of myelination of the nerve fibers of different regions of the cortex. McGraw (1946, 1963) has summarized some of the literature on postnatal cortical maturation, and deCrinis (1932) has studied the developmental state, in brains of infants come to autopsy at ages varying from 5 days to 13 years. This latter investigator reports that the maturation of Broca's speech area occurs more slowly in postnatal life than do the motor centers of the brain. The development of this speech center indeed is already behind that of the motor areas at birth, and during the first year this relative delay in maturation becomes even greater. At fourteen postnatal months the cellular maturation of Broca's area is not as great as that of the motor region five months earlier.

Walle J. H. Nauta, in a personal communication, reports that significant work in this important area of neurology is now being carried on by Poliakov and his associates in the laboratory of neurophysiology of the Academy of Sciences of the U.S.S.R., in the Moscow Brain Institute. Poliakov (1961) reports that what he calls the cortical projectional-associative connections develop functional maturity only by the second year of postnatal life. He says specifically:

The study of ontogenesis has shown that these regions of the cortex, which, apparently, constitute an essential part of the foundation of the human second signaling system (the brain mechanisms of speech, thought, and labor activity), terminate the cycle of their development later than all other regions, on the basis of the already formed systems of cortico-subcortical and cortico-cortical connections ensuring the capacity of the child to react to the first signals of the external environment.

The significance of the differential rate of the development of the specialized speech centers of the brain of man is attested in an interesting way by a comparison of the growth of vocalizing capacity, and the ability to respond to vocalizations, in man and in the chimpanzee. In this connection it may be noted that the brain of the chimpanzee reaches full anatomical maturity before that of man (Tilney, 1928). Kellogg and Kellogg (1933) have shown that in the first year of life a chimpanzee infant can learn to respond differentially to oral commands better than a human child. On the basis of what

has been said above, it may well be true that at this
time, in terms of maturation, it has a better brain to
make such responses possible than does the typical
human infant of the same age. When the child does
come to be able to use language in what has earlier been
termed a meaningful way, it is true, of course, that the
young human individual soon outdistances its ape com-
petitor in this and all other capacities related to what
we think of as effective mental life. It seems almost certain that these differences in capacity during early development must depend on differential brain maturation.
It is not without significance that Dr. and Mrs. Keith J.
Hayes (1951), who raised a chimpanzee baby, Viki, in
their home found that the animal learned haltingly to
say a few words, but never developed a truly effective
use of language, in spite of most intensive efforts on
their part in language training. However, Viki did learn
to respond to linguistic commands in a most adaptive
way. The difference between chimpanzee and child must
almost certainly be related to differences between human
and chimpanzee brains at different periods in their development.

These observations point to the fact that the normal
human infant's development of the ability to use meaningful words, even beyond the first year of life, is almost
certainly in some degree a function of the continuing
maturation of specific language mechanisms in its developing cortex.

It seems clear, therefore, that a fuller understanding
of the genesis of language in the individual will be

assisted by a more complete knowledge, based on histological and electrophysiological techniques, of the development in postnatal life of the basic brain regions that play a role in linguistic behavior. It may be pointed out further that such study must involve a coordination of both behavioral and anatomical investigations. This will be of value both to those who are interested in a theoretical knowledge of language growth and to those who are concerned with the care and possible cure of language defects in atypical or injured children, and even in such adult conditions as aphasia.

C. D. Mead (1913) set the average age for beginning to talk, in so-called normal children, as 15.3 months. This same investigator gave an average of 38.5 months for the beginning of true language in feeble-minded children. The interpretation of such results is not easy, for as McCarthy points out, studies show that it is by no means certain that a child who is late in talking is in any way mentally retarded.

It must be emphasized that it is not wise to generalize too easily on the basis of a few cases, concerning either early postnatal brain development or the growth of linguistic capacity in this period. The results so far secured, however, do point to the importance of a much more complete knowledge of cortical histology and physiology, correlated with recorded word utterance, in bringing about a better understanding of early human speech development. Such studies will be difficult and time consuming, but also rewarding.

REFERENCES

Armstrong, E. A. *Bird display and behavior*. New York: Oxford University Press, 1947.

Blanton, M. G. The behavior of the human infant during the first thirty days of life. *Psychol. Rev.*, 1917, **24**, 456-483.

Bühler, C., as cited in McCarthy, D. Language development in children. In L. Carmichael (Editor), *Manual of child psychology*. (2nd ed.) New York: John Wiley, 1954. Pp. 492-630.

Carmichael, L. The onset and early development of behavior. In L. Carmichael (Editor), *Manual of child psychology*. (2nd ed.) New York: John Wiley, 1954. Pp. 60-185.

Carmichael, L. *The making of modern mind: The emergence of mind in the animal series and the emergence of mind in the growing individual*. Houston: Elsevier Press, 1956.

Carmichael, L. Introduction to article by Jane Goodall, My life among wild chimpanzees. *Natl. Geogr. Mag.*, 1963, **124** (2), 272.

Crinis, M. de. Die entwicklung der Grosshirnrinde nach der Geburt in ihren Beziehungen zur intellektuellen Ausreifung des Kindes. *Wien. klin. Wschr.*, 1932, **45**, 1161-1165.

De Laguna, G. A. *Speech: its function and development*. New Haven: Yale University Press, 1927.

Feldman, W. M. *The principles of ante-natal and post-natal child physiology*. London: Longmans, 1920.

Frisch, K. v. *Ueber die "Sprache" der Bienen: Eine tierpsychologische Untersuchung*. Jena: Fischer, 1923.

Goodall, Jane. My life among wild chimpanzees. *Natl. Geogr. Mag.*, 1963, **124** (2), 278-308.

Graham, M. Intra-uterine crying. *Brit. med. J.*, 1919, **1**, 675.

Hayes, C. *The ape in our house*. New York: Harper, 1951.

Hermann, K. *Reading disability: A medical study of word-blindness and related handicaps*. Springfield, Ill.: Thomas, 1959.

Keller, H. *The story of my life*. New York: Doubleday & Page, 1913.

Kellogg, W. N., and Kellogg, L. A. *The ape and the child: A study of environmental influence upon early behavior.* New York: McGraw-Hill, 1933.

Mann, W. M. *Wild animals in and out of the zoo.* Washington, D.C.: Smithsonian Scientific Series, Vol. 6, 1930.

McCarthy, D. Language development in children. In L. Carmichael (Editor), *Manual of child psychology.* (2nd ed.) New York: John Wiley, 1954. Pp. 492-630.

McGraw, M. B. *Maturation of behavior.* In L. Carmichael (Editor), *Manual of child psychology.* (1st ed.) New York: John Wiley, 1946. Pp. 332-369.

McGraw, M. B. *The neuromuscular maturation of the human infant.* New York: Hafner, 1963.

Mead, C. D. The age of walking and talking in relation to general intelligence. *Ped. Sem.,* 1913, **20**, 460-484.

Minkowski, M. Ueber fruhzeitige Bewegungen. *Schweiz. med. Wschr.,* 1922, **52**, 721 and 751.

Penfield, W., and Rasmussen, T. *The cerebral cortex of man: A clinical study of localization of function.* New York: Macmillan, 1952.

Poliakov, G. I. Some results of research into the development of the neuronal structure of the cortical ends of the analyzers in man. *J. comp. Neurol.,* 1961, **117**, 197-212.

Preyer, W. *Mental development in the child.* (Transl. by H. W. Brown) New York: D. Appleton, 1893.

Rau, P., and Rau, N. Sex attraction and rhythmic periodicity in saturniid moths. *Trans. Acad. Sci., St. Louis,* 1929, **26**, 83-221.

Rawdon-Smith, A. F., Carmichael, L., and Wellman, B. Electrical responses from the cochlea of the fetal guinea pig. *J. exp. Psychol.,* 1938, **23**, 531-535.

Roeder, K. D. *Nerve cells and insect behavior.* Cambridge, Mass.: Harvard University Press, 1963.

Skinner, B. F. *Verbal behavior.* New York: Appleton-Century-Crofts, 1957.

Tilney, F. *The brain from ape to man.* 2 vols. New York: P. B. Hoeber, 1928.

Tinbergen, N. *The study of instinct.* Oxford: Clarendon, 1951.

Warden, C. J., Jenkins, T. N., and Warner, L. H. *Plants and invertebrates,* Vol. II of *Comparative psychology: A comprehensive treatise.* New York: Ronald, 1940.

Yerkes, R. M., and Yerkes, A. W. Social behavior in infrahuman primates. In C. Murchison (Editor), *Handbook of social psychology.* Worcester, Mass.: Clark University Press, 1935. Pp. 973-1033.

E D M U N D   L E A C H [*]

Anthropological Aspects of Language: Animal Categories and Verbal Abuse

The central theme of my essay is the classical anthropological topic of 'taboo.' This theme, in this guise, does not form part of the conventional field of discourse of experimental psychologists; yet the argument that I shall present has its psychological equivalents. When psychologists debate about the mechanism of 'forgetting' they often introduce the concept of 'interference,' the idea that there is a tendency to repress concepts that have some kind of semantic overlap (Postman, 1961). The thesis which I present depends upon a converse hypothesis, namely, that we can only arrive at semantically distinct verbal concepts if we repress the boundary percepts that lie between them.

To discuss the anthropological aspects of language within the confines of space allotted to me here is like

* University of Cambridge, England.

writing a history of England in thirty lines. I propose
to tackle a specific theme, not a general one. For the
anthropologist, language is a part of culture, not a thing
in itself. Most of the anthropologist's problems are concerned with human communication. Language is one
means of communication, but customary acts of behavior are also a means of communication, and the
anthropologist feels that he can, and should, keep both
modes of communication in view at the same time.

Language and Taboo

This is a symposium about language but my theme is
one of nonlanguage. Instead of discussing things that are
said and done, I want to talk about things that are not
said and done. My theme is that of taboo, expression
which is inhibited.

Anthropological and psychological literature alike
are crammed with descriptions and learned explanations
of apparently irrational prohibitions and inhibitions.
Such 'taboo' may be either behavioral or linguistic, and
it deserves note that the protective sanctions are very
much the same in either case. If at this moment I were
really anxious to get arrested by the police, I might strip
naked or launch into a string of violent obscenities:
either procedure would be equally effective.

Linguistic taboos and behavioral taboos are not only
sanctioned in the same way, they are very much muddled
up: sex behavior and sex words, for example. But this
association of deed and word is not so simple as might
appear. The relationship is not necessarily causal. It is

not the case that certain kinds of behavior are taboo and that, therefore, the language relating to such behavior becomes taboo. Sometimes words may be taboo in themselves for linguistic (phonemic) reasons, and the causal link, if any, is then reversed; a behavioral taboo comes to reflect a prior verbal taboo. In this paper I shall only touch upon the fringe of this complex subject.

A familiar type of purely linguistic taboo is the pun. A pun occurs when we make a joke by confusing two apparently different meanings of the same phonemic pattern. The pun seems funny or shocking because it challenges a taboo which ordinarily forbids us to recognize that the sound pattern is ambiguous. In many cases such verbal taboos have social as well as linguistic aspects. In English, though not I think in American, the word *queen* has a homonym *quean*. The words are phonetically indistinguishable (KWĪN). Queen is the consort of King or even a female sovereign in her own right; quean which formerly meant a prostitute now usually denotes a homosexual male. In the nonhuman world we have queen bees and brood queen cats, both indicating a splendid fertility, but a quean is a barren cow. Although these two words pretend to be different, indeed opposites, they really denote the same idea. A queen is a female of abnormal status in a positive virtuous sense; a quean is a person of depraved character or uncertain sex, a female of abnormal status in a negative sinful sense. Yet their common abnormality turns both into 'supernatural' beings; so also, in metaphysics, the contraries God and the Devil are both supernatural beings. In this case, then, the taboo which allows us to separate the two ambiguous concepts, so that we can talk of queens without thinking of queans, and vice versa, is simultaneously both linguistic *and* social.

We should note that the taboo operates so as to distinguish two identical phonemic patterns; it does not operate so as to suppress the pattern altogether. We are not inhibited from saying KWIN. Yet the very similar phonemic pattern produced by shifting the dental N to bilabial M and shortening the medial vowel (KWĬM) is one of the most unprintable obscenities in the English language. Some American informants have assured me that this word has been so thoroughly suppressed that it has not crossed the Atlantic at all, but this does not seem entirely correct as there is dictionary evidence to the contrary.* It is hard to talk about the unsayable but I hope I have made my initial point. Taboo is simultaneously both behavioral and linguistic, both social and psychological. As an anthropologist, I am particularly concerned with the social aspects of taboo. Analytical psychologists of various schools are particularly concerned with the individual taboos which center in the oral, anal, and genital functions. Experimental psychologists may concern themselves with essentially the same

* The Oxford English Dictionary says nothing of the obscenity but records *Quim* as a 'late Scottish variant' of the now wholly obsolete *Queme* = 'pleasant.' Partridge (1949) prints the word in full (whereas he balks at f*ck and c*nt). His gloss is 'the female pudend' and he gives *queme* as a variant. Funk and Wagnalls, and Webster, latest editions, both ignore the term, but H. Wentworth and S. B. Flexner (1961) give:

quim n. 1 = queen; 2 (taboo) = the vagina.

That this phonemic pattern is, in fact, penumbral to the more permissible *queen* is thus established.

The American dictionaries indicate that the range of meanings of *queen (quean)* are the same as in England, but the distinction of spelling is not firmly maintained.

kind of phenomenon when they examine the process of forgetting, or various kinds of muscular inhibition. But all these varieties of repression are so meshed into the web of language that discussion of any one of the three frames, anthropological, psychological, or linguistic, must inevitably lead on to some consideration of the other two.

Animal Categories and Verbal Obscenities

In the rest of this paper I shall have relatively little to say about language in a direct sense, but this is because of the nature of my problem. I shall be discussing the connection between animal categories and verbal obscenities. Plainly it is much easier to talk about the animals than about the obscenities! The latter will mostly be just off stage. But the hearer (and the reader) should keep his wits about him. Just as queen is dangerously close to the unsayable, so also there are certain very familiar animals which are, as it were, only saved by a phoneme from sacrilege or worse. In seventeenth century English witchcraft trials it was very commonly asserted that the Devil appeared in the form of a Dog— that is, God backwards. In England we still employ this same metathesis when we refer to a clergyman's collar as a 'dog collar' instead of a 'God collar.' So also it needs only a slight vowel shift in *fox* to produce the obscene *fux*. No doubt there is a sense in which such facts as these can be deemed linguistic accidents, but they are accidents which have a functional utility in the way we use our language. As I shall show presently, there

are good sociological reasons why the English categories
dog and *fox,* like the English category *queen (quean),*
should evoke taboo associations in their phonemic
vicinity.

As an anthropologist I do not profess to understand
the psychological aspects of the taboo phenomenon.
I do not understand what happens when a word or a
phrase or a detail of behavior is subject to repression.
But I can observe what happens. In particular I can
observe that when verbal taboos are broken the result
is a specific social phenomenon which affects both the
actor and his hearers in a specific describable way. I
need not elaborate. This phenomenon is what we mean
by obscenity. Broadly speaking, the language of obscenity falls into three categories: (1) dirty words—usually
referring to sex and excretion; (2) blasphemy and profanity; (3) animal abuse—in which a human being
is equated with an animal of another species.

These categories are not in practice sharply distinguished. Thus the word 'bloody,' which is now a kind of
all-purpose mildly obscene adjective, is felt by some
to be associated with menstrual blood and is thus a
'dirty' word, but it seems to be historically derived from
profanity—'By our Lady.' On the other hand, the simple
expletive 'damn!'—now presumed to be short for 'dam-
nation!'—and thus a profanity—was formerly 'god-
dam' (God's animal mother) an expression combining
blasphemy with animal abuse. These broad categories
of obscenity seem to occur in most languages.

The dirty words present no problem. Psychologists
have adequate and persuasive explanations of why the

central focus or the crudest obscenity should ordinarily lie in sex and excretion. The language of profanity and blasphemy also presents no problem. Any theory about the sacredness of supernatural beings is likely to imply a concept of sacrilege which in turn explains the emotions aroused by profanity and blasphemy. But animal abuse seems much less easily accounted for. Why should expressions like 'you son of a bitch' or 'you swine' carry the connotations that they do, when 'you son of a kangaroo' or 'you polar bear' have no meaning whatever?

I write as an anthropologist, and for an anthropologist this theme of animal abuse has a very basic interest. When an animal name is used in this way as an imprecation, it indicates that the name itself is credited with potency. It clearly signifies that the animal category is in some way taboo and sacred. Thus, for an anthropologist, animal abuse is part of a wide field of study which includes animal sacrifice and totemism.

Relation of Edibility and Social Valuation of Animals

In his ethnographic studies the anthropologist observes that, in any particular cultural situation, some animals are the focus of ritual attitudes whereas others are not; moreover, the intensity of the ritual involvement of individual species varies greatly. It is never at all obvious why this should be so, but one fact that is commonly relevant and always needs to be taken into consideration is the edibility of the species in question.

One hypothesis which underlies the rest of this paper

is that animal abuse is in some way linked with what
Radcliffe-Brown called the ritual value of the animal
category concerned. I further assume that this ritual
value is linked in some as yet undetermined way with
taboos and rules concerning the killing and eating of
these and other animals. For the purposes of illustration,
I shall confine my attention to categories of the English
language. I postulate, however, that the principles which
I adduce are very general, though not necessarily universal. In illustration of this, I discuss as an appendix
to my main argument the application of my thesis to
categories of the Kachin language spoken by certain
highland groups in northeast Burma.

Taboo is not a genuine English word, but a category
imported from Polynesia. Its meaning is not precisely
defined in conventional English usage. Anthropologists
commonly use it to refer to prohibitions which are explicit and which are supported by feelings of sin and
supernatural sanction at a conscious level; incest regu-
lations provide a typical example; the rules recorded
in Leviticus XI, verses 4–47, which prohibited the Israel-
ites from eating a wide variety of 'unclean beasts,' are
another. In this paper, however, I shall use the concept
of food taboo in a more general sense, so that it covers
all classes of food prohibition, explicit and implicit,
conscious and unconscious.

Cultural and Linguistic Determination of Food Values

The physical environment of any human society contains a vast range of materials which are both edible

and nourishing, but, in most cases, only a small part of this edible environment will actually be classified as potential food. Such classification is a matter of language and culture, not of nature. It is a classification that is of great practical importance, and it is felt to be so. *Our* classification is not only correct, it is morally right and a mark of our superiority. The fact that frogs' legs are a gourmet's delicacy in France but not food at all in England provokes the English to refer to Frenchmen as Frogs with implications of withering contempt.

As a consequence of such cultural discriminations, the edible part of the environment usually falls into three main categories:

1. Edible substances that are recognized as food and consumed as part of the normal diet.

2. Edible substances that are recognized as possible food, but that are prohibited or else allowed to be eaten only under special (ritual) conditions. These are substances which are *consciously tabooed*.

3. Edible substances that by culture and language are not recognized as food at all. These substances are *unconsciously tabooed*.

Now in the ordinary way when anthropologists discuss food taboos they are thinking only of my second category; they have in mind such examples as the Jewish prohibitions against pork, the Brahmin prohibition against beef, the Christian attitude to sacramental bread and wine. But my third category of edible substances that are not classed as food deserves equal attention. The nature of the taboo in the two cases is quite distinct.

The Jewish prohibition against pork is a ritual matter and explicit. It says, in effect, "pork is a food, but Jews must not eat it." The Englishman's objection to eating dog is quite as strong but rests on a different premise. It depends on a categorical assumption: "dog is not food."

In actual fact, of course, dogs are perfectly edible, and in some parts of the world they are bred for eating. For that matter human beings are edible, though to an Englishman the very thought is disgusting. I think most Englishmen would find the idea of eating dog equally disgusting and in a similar way. I believe that this latter disgust is largely a matter of verbal categories. There are contexts in colloquial English in which man and dog may be thought of as beings of the same kind. Man and dog are 'companions'; the dog is 'the friend of man.' On the other hand man and food are antithetical categories. Man is not food, so dog cannot be food either.

Of course our linguistic categories are not always tidy and logical, but the marginal cases, which at first appear as exceptions to some general rule, are often especially interesting. For example, the French eat horse. In England, although horsemeat may be fed to dogs, it is officially classed as unfit for human consumption. Horsemeat may not be sold in the same shop that handles ordinary butchers' meat, and in London where, despite English prejudice, there are low foreigners who actually eat the stuff, they must buy it in a shop labeled *charcuterie* and not *butcher*! This I suggest is quite consistent with the very special attitude which Englishmen adopt toward both dogs and horses. Both are sacred supernatural creatures surrounded by feelings that are ambiguously those of awe and horror. This kind of attitude is comparable to a less familiar but much more improbable statutory rule which lays down that Swan and Sturgeon may only be eaten by members of the Royal Family, except once a year when Swan may be eaten by the members of St. John's College, Cambridge! As the Editor of *The New Yorker* is fond of telling us, "There will always be an England!"

Plainly all such rules, prejudices, and conventions are of social origin; yet the social taboos have their linguistic counterparts and, as I shall presently show, these accidents of etymological history fit together in a quite surprising way. Certainly in its linguistic aspects horse looks innocent enough, but so do dog and fox. However, in most English colloquial, horse is *'orse* or *'oss* and in this form it shares with its companion *ass* an uncomfortable approximation to the human posterior.*

The problem then is this. The English treat certain animals as taboo—sacred. This sacredness is manifested in various ways, partly behavioral, as when we are forbidden to eat flesh of the animal concerned, partly linguistic, as when a phonemic pattern penumbral to that of the animal category itself is found to be a focus of

---

* English and American taboos are different. The English spell the animal *ass* and the buttocks *arse* but, according to Partridge (1949), *arse* was considered almost unprintable between 1700 and 1930 (though it appears in the O.E.D.). Webster's Third Edition spells both words as *ass*, noting that *arse* is a more polite variant of the latter word, which also has the obscene meaning, sexual intercourse. Funk and Wagnalls (1952) distinguish *ass* (animal) and *arse* (buttocks) and do not cross reference. Wentworth and Flexner (1961) give only *ass* but give three taboo meanings, the rectum, the buttocks, and the vagina.

obscenity, profanity, etc. Can we get any insight into
why certain creatures should be treated this way?

Taboo and the Distinctiveness of Namable Categories

Before I proceed further, let me give you an outline
of a general theory of taboo which I find particularly
satisfactory in my work as an anthropologist. It is a
theory which seems to me to fit in well with the psychological and linguistic facts. In the form in which I present it here, it is a 'Leach theory' but it has several
obvious derivations, especially Radcliffe-Brown's discussions of ritual value, Mary Douglas's thinking (still
largely unpublished) on anomalous animals, and Lévi-
Strauss's version of the Hegelian-Marxist dialectic in
which the sacred elements of myth are shown to be
factors that mediate contradictories.

I postulate that the physical and social environment
of a young child is perceived as a continuum. It does
not contain any intrinsically separate 'things.' The
child, in due course, is taught to impose upon this environment a kind of discriminating grid which serves
to distinguish the world as being composed of a large
number of separate things, each labeled with a name.
This world is a representation of our language categories, not vice versa. Because my mother tongue is
English, it seems self evident that *bushes* and *trees* are
different kinds of things. I would not think this unless I
had been taught that it was the case.

Now if each individual has to learn to construct his
own environment in this way, it is crucially important

that the basic discriminations should be clear-cut and unambiguous. There must be absolutely no doubt about the difference between *me* and *it*, or between *we* and *they*. But how can such certainty of discrimination be achieved if our normal perception displays only a continuum? A diagram may help. Our uninhibited (untrained) perception recognizes a continuum (Figure 1).

───────────

Fig. 1. The line is a schematic representation of continuity in nature. There are no gaps in the physical world.

We are taught that the world consists of 'things' distinguished by names; therefore we have to train our perception to recognize a discontinuous environment (Figure 2).

── ── ── ──

Fig. 2. Schematic representation of what in nature is named. Many aspects of the physical world remain unnamed in natural languages.

We achieve this second kind of trained perception by means of a simultaneous use of language and taboo. Language gives us the names to distinguish the things; taboo inhibits the recognition of those parts of the continuum which separate the things (Figure 3).

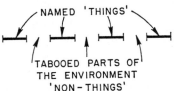

Fig. 3. The relationship of tabooed objects to the world of names.

The same kind of argument may also be represented by a simplified Venn diagram employing two circles only. Let there be a circle p representing a particular verbal category. Let this be intersected by another circle $\sim p$ representing the 'environment' of p, from which it is desired to distinguish p. If by a fiction we impose a taboo upon any consideration of the overlap area that is common to both circles, then we shall be able to persuade ourselves that p and $\sim p$ are wholly distinct, and the logic of binary discrimination will be satisfied (Figure 4).

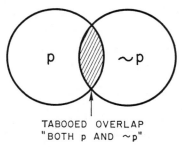

TABOOED OVERLAP
"BOTH p AND ~p"

Fig. 4. The relationship between ambiguity and taboo.

Language then does more than provide us with a classification of things; it actually molds our environment; it places each individual at the center of a social space which is ordered in a logical and reassuring way.

In this paper I shall be specially concerned with verbal category sets which discriminate areas of social space in terms of 'distance from Ego (self).' For example, consider the three sets (a), (b), (c).

(a)   Self ·· Sister ·· Cousin ·· Neighbor ·· Stranger
(b)   Self ·· House ·· Farm ·· Field ·· Far (**Remote**)

(c) Self ·· Pet ·· Livestock ·· 'Game' ·· Wild
     Animal

For each of these three sets, the words, thus arranged,
indicate categories that are progressively more remote
from Self, but I believe that there is more to it than
that. I hope to be able to show that, if we denote these
word sets as

(a)	A1	B1	C1	D1	E1
(b)	A2	B2	C2	D2	E2
(c)	A3	B3	C3	D3	E3

then the relational statement A1:B1:C1:D1:E1 is the
same as the relational statement A2:B2:C2:D2:E2 or
the relational statement A3:B3:C3:D3:E3. In other
words, the way we employ the words in set (c), a set
of animals, allows us to make statements about the
human relationships which belong to set (a).

But I am going too fast. Let us go back to my theory
of taboo. If we operate in the way I have suggested,
so that we are only able to perceive the environment
as composed of separate things by suppressing our
recognition of the nonthings which fill the interstices,
then of course what is suppressed becomes especially
interesting. Quite apart from the fact that all scientific
enquiry is devoted to 'discovering' those parts of the
environment that lie on the borders of what is 'already
known,' we have the phenomenon, which is variously
described by anthropologists and psychologists, in which
whatever is taboo is a focus not only of special interest
but also of anxiety. Whatever is taboo is sacred, valu-

able, important, powerful, dangerous, untouchable, filthy, unmentionable.

I can illustrate my point by mentioning diametrically contrasted areas where this approach to taboo fits in well with the observable facts. First, the exudations of the human body are universally the objects of intense taboo—in particular, feces, urine, semen, menstrual blood, hair clippings, nail parings, body dirt, spittle, mother's milk.* This fits the theory. Such substances are ambiguous in the most fundamental way. The child's first and continuing problem is to determine the initial boundary. "What am I, as against the world?" "Where is the edge of me?" In this fundamental sense, feces, urine, semen, and so forth, are both me and not me. So strong is the resulting taboo that, even as an adult addressing an adult audience, I cannot refer to these substances by the monosyllabic words which I used as a child but must mention them only in Latin. But let us be clear, it is not simply that these substances are felt to be dirty—they are powerful; throughout the world it is precisely such substances that are the prime ingredients of magical 'medicines.'

At the opposite extreme, consider the case of the sanctity of supernatural beings. Religious belief is everywhere tied in with the discrimination between living and dead. Logically, *life* is simply the binary antithesis of *death*; the two concepts are the opposite sides of

---

* An interesting and seemingly unique partial exception to this catalogue is 'tears.' Tears can acquire sacredness, in that the tears of Saints have been turned into relics and tears are proper at sacred situations, e.g., funerals, but tears are not, I think, felt to be dirty or contaminating after the manner of other exudations.

the same penny; we cannot have either without the other. But religion always tries to separate the two. To do this it creates a hypothetical 'other world' which is the antithesis of 'this world.' In this world life and death are inseparable; in the other world they are separate. This world is inhabited by imperfect mortal men; the other world is inhabited by immortal nonmen (gods). The category god is thus constructed as the binary antithesis of man. But this is inconvenient. A remote god in another world may be logically sensible, but it is emotionally unsatisfying. To be useful, gods must be near at hand, so religion sets about reconstructing a continuum between this world and the other world. But note how it is done. The gap between the two logically distinct categories, this world/other world, is filled in with tabooed ambiguity. The gap is bridged by supernatural beings of a highly ambiguous kind—incarnate deities, virgin mothers, supernatural monsters which are half man/half beast. These marginal, ambiguous creatures are specifically credited with the power of mediating between gods and men. They are the object of the most intense taboos, more sacred than the gods themselves. In an objective sense, as distinct from theoretical theology, it is the Virgin Mary, human mother of God, who is the principal object of devotion in the Catholic church.

So here again it is the ambiguous categories that attract the maximum interest and the most intense feelings of taboo. The general theory is that taboo applies to categories which are anomalous with respect to clearcut category oppositions. If A and B are two verbal categories, such that B is defined as "what A is not" and vice versa, and there is a third category C which mediates this distinction, in that C shares attributes of both A and B, then C will be taboo.

But now let us return to a consideration of English animal categories and food taboos.

Animal and Food Names in English

How do we speakers of English classify animals, and how is this classification related to the matters of killing and eating and verbal abuse?

The basic discrimination seems to rest in three words:

Fish   creatures that live in water. A very elastic category, it includes even crustacea—'shell fish.'

Birds   two-legged creatures with wings which lay eggs. (They do not necessarily fly, e.g., penguins, ostriches.)

Beasts   four-legged mammals living on land.

Consider Table 1. All creatures that are edible are fish or birds or beasts. There is a large residue of creatures, rated as either *reptiles* or *insects*, but the whole of this ambiguous residue is rated as not food. All reptiles and insects seem to be thought of as evil enemies of mankind and liable to the most ruthless extermination. Only the bee is an exception here, and significantly the bee is often credited with quite superhuman powers of intelligence and organization. The hostile taboo is applied most strongly to creatures that are most

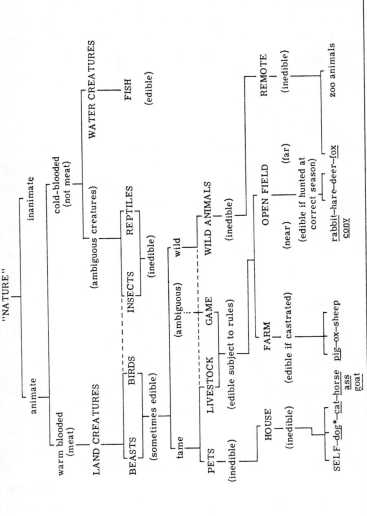

"NATURE"

animate — inanimate

warm blooded (meat) — cold-blooded (not meat)

LAND CREATURES — WATER CREATURES

(ambiguous creatures) — FISH (edible)

BEASTS (sometimes edible) — BIRDS — INSECTS (inedible) — REPTILES (inedible)

tame — wild

(ambiguous)

PETS (inedible) — LIVESTOCK (edible subject to rules) — GAME (edible if castrated) — WILD ANIMALS (inedible)

HOUSE (inedible) — FARM — OPEN FIELD — REMOTE (inedible)

SELF—dog*—cat—horse — ass — goat

pig—ox—sheep

('near') — ('far')

rabbit—hare—deer—fox cony (edible if hunted at correct season)

zoo animals

* The species underlined on the bottom line are those which appear to be specially loaded with taboo values, as indicated by their use in obscenity and abuse or by metaphysical associations or by the intrusion of euphemism.

anomalous in respect of the major categories, e.g. snakes—land animals with no legs which lay eggs.

The fact that birds and beasts are warm-blooded and that they engage in sexual intercourse in a 'normal' way makes them to some extent akin to man. This is shown by the fact that the concept of *cruelty* is applicable to birds and beasts but not to fish. The slaughter of farm animals for food must be carried out by 'humane' methods;* in England we even have humane rat traps! But it is quite proper to kill a lobster by dropping it alive into boiling water. Where religious food taboos apply, they affect only the warm-blooded, near human, meat of birds and beasts; hence Catholics may eat fish on Fridays. In England the only common fish subject to killing and eating restrictions is the salmon. This is an anomalous fish in at least two respects; it is red-blooded and it is simultaneously both a sea fish and a fresh water fish. But the mammalian *beasts* are much closer to man than the egg-laying *birds*. The Society for the Prevention of Cruelty to Animals, the Anti-Vivisection Society, Our Dumb Friends League and such organizations devote most of their attention to four-footed creatures, and as time is short I shall do the same.

Structure of Food and Kinship Terminologies

Anthropologists have noted again and again that there is a universal tendency to make ritual and verbal associations between eating and sexual intercourse. It is

---

* The word *humane* has become distinguished from *human* only since the 17th century.

thus a plausible hypothesis that the way in which animals are categorized with regard to edibility will have some correspondence to the way in which human beings are categorized with regard to sex relations.

Upon this matter the anthropologists have assembled a vast amount of comparative data. The following generalization is certainly not a universal, but it has a very wide general validity. From the point of view of any male SELF, the young women of his social world will fall into four major classes:

1. Those who are very close—'true sisters,' always a strongly incestuous category.

2. Those who are kin but not very close—'first cousins' in English society, 'clan sisters' in many types of systems having unilineal descent and a segmentary lineage organization. As a rule, marriage with this category is either prohibited or strongly disapproved, but premarital sex relations may be tolerated or even expected.

3. Neighbors (friends) who are not kin, potential affines. This is the category from which SELF will ordinarily expect to obtain a wife. This category contains also potential enemies, friendship and enmity being alternating aspects of the same structural relationship.

4. Distant strangers—who are known to exist but with whom no social relations of any kind are possible.

Now the English put most of their animals into four very comparable categories:

1. Those who are very close—'pets,' always strongly inedible.

2. Those who are tame but not very close—'farm animals,' mostly edible but only if immature or castrated. We seldom eat a sexually intact, mature farm beast.*

3. Field animals, 'game'—a category toward which we alternate friendship and hostility. Game animals live under human protection but they are not tame. They are edible in sexually intact form, but are killed only at set seasons of the year in accordance with set hunting rituals.

4. Remote wild animals—not subject to human control, inedible.

Thus presented, there appears to be a set of equivalents

incest prohibition	inedible
marriage prohibition coupled with premarital sex relations	castration coupled with edibility
marriage alliance, friend/enemy ambiguity	edible in sexually intact form; alternating friendship/hostility
no sex relations with remote strangers	remote wild animals are inedible

That this correspondence between the categories of sexual accessibility and the categories of edibility is rather more than just an accident is shown by a further accident of a linguistic kind. The archaic legal expres-

---

* Two reasons are usually offered for castrating farm animals. The first, which is valid, is that the castrated animal is more amenable to handling. The second, which I am assured is scientifically invalid, is that a castrated animal produces more succulent meat in a shorter time.

sion for game was beasts of venery. The term venery had the alternative meanings, hunting and sexual indulgence.

A similar accident yields the phonemic resemblance between *venery* and *venerate* which is reminiscent of that between *quean* and *queen*. Sex and authority are both sources of taboo (respect) but in contrary senses.

A fifth major category of English animals which cuts across the others, and is significantly taboo-loaded, is vermin. The dictionary definition of this word is comprehensively ambiguous:

mammals and birds injurious to game, crops, etc.; foxes, weasels, rats, mice, moles, owls, noxious insects, fleas, bugs, lice, parasitic worms, vile persons.

Vermin may also be described as *pests* (i.e., plagues). Although vermin and pests are intrinsically inedible, rabbits and pigeon, which are pests when they attack crops, may also be classed as game and then become edible. The same two species also become edible when kept under restraint as farm animals. I shall have more to say about rabbits presently.

Before we go further, let me review the latest part of my argument in rather different form. The thesis is that we make binary distinctions and then mediate the distinction by creating an ambiguous (and taboo-loaded) intermediate category. Thus:

p	both p and $\sim p$	$\sim p$
man	'man-animal'	not man
(not animal)	('pets')	(animal)
TAME	GAME	WILD
(friendly)	(friendly/hostile)	(hostile)

We have already given some indication that ritual value (taboo) attaches in a marked way to the intermediate categories *pets* and *game*, and I shall have more to say about this, but we shall find that even more intense taboo attitudes are revealed when we come to consider creatures which would only fit into the interstices of the above tabulation, e.g., goats, pigs, and horses which are not quite pets, rabbits which are not quite game, and foxes which are wild but treated like game in some respects (see bottom of Table 1).

In Table 2 are listed the more familiar names of the more familiar English animals. These name sets possess certain linguistic characteristics.

Nearly all the house pets, farm, and field (game) animals have monosyllabic names: dog, cat, bull, cow, ox, and so on, whereas among the more remote wild beasts monosyllables are rare. The vocabulary is most elaborated in the farm category and most attenuated in the inedible house-pet and wild-beast categories.

Thus farm animals have separate terms for (1) an intact male, (2) an intact female, (3) a suckling, (4) an immature female, (5) a castrated male (e.g., bull, cow, calf, heifer, bullock, with local variants). This is not surprising in view of the technical requirements of farming, but it seems odd that the pet vocabulary should be so restricted. Thus dog has only: dog, bitch, pup, and of these bitch is largely taboo and seldom used; cat has only: cat, kitten.

If sex discrimination must be made among pets, one can say 'bitch' and 'tom cat.' This implies that a dog is otherwise presumed male and a cat female. Indeed cat and dog are paired terms, and seem to serve as a paradigm for quarreling husband and wife.

Among the field animals all males are *bucks* and all females *does*. Among the wild animals, in a small number of species we distinguish the young as *cubs*. In a smaller number we distinguish the female as a variant of the male: tiger—tigress; lion—lioness; but most are sexless. Fox is a very special case, exceptional in all respects. It is a monosyllable, the male is a *dog*, the female a *vixen*, the young a *cub*. Elephants and some other 'zoo animals' are distinguished as bulls, cows, and calves, a direct borrowing from the farm-animal set.

A curious usage suggests that we are ashamed of killing any animal of substantial size. When dead, bullock becomes *beef*, pig becomes *pork*, sheep becomes *mutton*, calf becomes *veal*, and deer becomes *venison*. But smaller animals stay as they are: lamb, hare, and rabbit, and all birds are the same alive or dead. Goats are 'nearly pets' and correspondingly (for the English) goat meat is nearly inedible. An English housewife would be outraged if she thought that her mutton was goat!

Animal Abuse and Eating Habits

Most of the monosyllables denoting familiar animals may be stretched to describe the qualities of human beings. Such usage is often abusive but not always so. Bitch, cat, pig, swine, ass, goat, cur (dog) are insults; but lamb, duck, and cock are friendly, even affectionate. Close animals may also serve as near obscene euphe-

Table 2
ENGLISH SUBCATEGORIES OF FAMILIAR ANIMALS

	Female	Male	Infant	Young male[a]	Young female[a]	Castrated male	Baby language	Carcass meat
Dog	Bitch		Puppy				Bow wow	
Hound			Whelp				Doggy	
Cat		(Tom)	Kitten				Pussy	
Goat	(Nanny)	(Billy)	Kid				?	(Mutton)
Pig	Sow	Boar	Piglet	Hogget[b]	Gilt	Hog[c] Porker	Piggy	Pork, bacon, ham
Ass							Ee-yaw	
Horse[d]	Mare	Stallion	Foal	Colt	Filly	Gelding	Gee-gee	
Cow (ox)[e]	Cow	Bull	Calf		Heifer	Steer Bullock	Moo-cow	Veal; beef[f]
Sheep	Ewe	Ram	Lamb	Teg			Baa-lamb	Mutton
Fowl	Hen	Cock	Chick	Cockerel	Pullet	Capon	?	Chicken
Duck	Duck	Drake	Duckling				Quack-quack	
Goose	Goose	Gander	Gosling					
Pigeon			Squab					
Rabbit	Doe	Buck					Bunny	
Hare	Doe	Buck	Leveret					
Deer	Doe Hind	Buck Stag[g]						Venison
Swan			Cygnet					
Fox	Vixen	Dog	Cub[h]					

a Other sex distinctions:

Most birds other than duck and goose may be distinguished as cocks and hens.

The whale, walrus, elephant, moose, and certain other large animals are distinguished as bulls and cows.

Lion and tiger are presumed male since they have feminine forms lioness, tigress.

The female of certain other species is marked by prefixing the pronoun 'she'; thus, she-bear.

b Hogget—a boar in its second year. The term may also apply to a young horse (colt) or to a young sheep (teg).

c Hog—may also refer to pigs in general as also *swine*.

d Note also *pony*, a small horse suitable for children.

e Ox (Oxen)—properly the term for the species in general, but now archaic and where used at all refers to a castrated male. The common species term is now *cow* (*cows*) or *cattle*. Cattle is in origin the same as capital = 'live stock.' The archaic plural of *cow* is *kine* (cf. *kin*).

f Beef—in singular = dead meat, but *beeves* plural refers to live animals = bullocks.

g Hart—an old stag with sur-royal antlers.

h Cub (whelp)—includes young of many wild animals: tiger, bear, otter, etc.

misms for unmentionable parts of the human anatomy. Thus cock = penis, pussy = female pubic hair, and, in America, ass = arse.

The principle that the close, familiar animals are denoted by monosyllables is so general that the few exceptions invite special attention. The use of phonetically complex terms for 'close' animals seems always to be the result of a euphemistic replacement of a tabooed word. Thus *donkey* has replaced *ass*, and *rabbit* has replaced *coney*. This last term now survives only in the fur trade where it is pronounced to rhyme with Tony, but its etymological derivation is from Latin *cuniculus*, and the 18th century rabbit was a cunny, awkwardly close to *cunt*, which only became printable in English with the licensed publication of *Lady Chatterley's Lover*. It is interesting that while the adult cunny has switched to the innocuous rabbit, baby language has retained bunny. I gather that in contemporary New York a Bunny Club has at least a superficial resemblance to a London eighteenth century Cunny House.*

Some animals seem to carry an unfair load of abuse. Admittedly the pig is a general scavenger but so, by nature, is the dog and it is hardly rational that we should label the first 'filthy' while making a household pet of the second. I suspect that we feel a rather special guilt about our pigs. After all, sheep provide wool,

---

* In general, birds fall outside the scope of this paper, but while considering the ambiguities introduced by the accidents of linguistic homonyms we may note that all edible birds are *fowl* (i.e., foul = filthy); that *pigeon* has replaced *dove*, perhaps because of the association of the latter with the Holy Ghost; and that the word *squabble* (a noisy quarrel, particularly between married couples) is derived from *squab*, a young pigeon.

cows provide milk, chickens provide eggs, but we rear pigs for the sole purpose of killing and eating them, and this is rather a shameful thing, a shame which quickly attaches to the pig itself. Besides which, under English rural conditions, the pig in his backyard pigsty was, until very recently, much more nearly a member of the household than any of the other edible animals. Pigs, like dogs, were fed from the leftovers of their human masters' kitchens. To kill and eat such a commensal associate is sacrilege indeed!

In striking contrast to the monosyllabic names of the close animals, we find that at the other end of the scale there is a large class of truly wild animals, most of which the ordinary individual sees only in a zoo. Such creatures are not classed as potential food at all. To distinguish these strangers as lying outside our English social system, we have given them very long semi-Latin names—elephant, hippopotamus, rhinoceros, and so forth. This is not due to any scholastic perversity; these words have been a part of the vernacular for a thousand years or so.

The intermediate category of fully sexed, tame-wild, field animals which we may hunt for food, but only in accordance with set rules at special seasons of the year, is in England now much reduced in scope. It now comprises certain birds (e.g., grouse, pheasant, partridge), hares, and, in some places, deer. As indicated already, rabbits and pigeons are both marginal to this category. Since all these creatures are protected for part of the year in order that they may be killed in the other, the collective name *game* is most appropriate. Social anthropologists have coined the expression *joking relation-ship* for a somewhat analogous state of affairs which is frequently institutionalized between affinally related groups among human beings.

Just as the obscene rabbit, which is ambiguously game or vermin, occupies an intermediate status between the farm and field categories (Table 1), the fox occupies the borderline between edible field and inedible wild animals. In England the hunting and killing of foxes is a barbarous ritual surrounded by extraordinary and fantastic taboos. The intensity of feeling aroused by these performances almost baffles the imagination. All attempts to interfere with such customs on the grounds of 'cruelty' have failed miserably. Some aspects of fox-hunting are linguistic and thus directly relevant to my theme. We find, for example, as commonly occurs in other societies in analogous contexts, that the sacredness of the situation is marked by language inversions, the use of special terms for familiar objects, and so on.

Thus foxes are hunted by packs of dogs and, at the conclusion of the ritual killing, the fox has its head and tail cut off, which are then preserved as trophies, but none of this may be said in plain language. It is the fox itself that can be spoken of as a *dog*, the dogs are described as *hounds*, the head of the fox is a *mask*, its tail a *brush*, and so on. It is considered highly improper to use any other words for these things.

Otters, stags, and hares are also sometimes hunted in a comparable ritual manner, and here again the hunting dogs change their identity, becoming either hounds or beagles. All of which reinforces my original hypothesis that the category *dog*, in English, is something very special indeed.

The implication of all this is that if we arrange the familiar animals in a series according to their social distance from the human SELF (Table 1, bottom) then we can see that the occurrence of taboo (ritual value), as indicated by different types and intensities of killing and eating restrictions, verbal abuse, metaphysical associations, ritual performance, the intrusion of euphemism, etc., is not just randomly distributed. The varieties of taboo are located at intervals across the chart in such a way as to break up the continuum into sections. Taboo serves to separate the SELF from the world, and then the world itself is divided into zones of social distance corresponding here to the words farm, field, and remote.

I believe that this kind of analysis is more than just an intellectual game; it can help us to understand a wide variety of our nonrational behavior. For example, anyone familiar with the literature will readily perceive that English witchcraft beliefs depended upon a confusion of precisely the categories to which I have here drawn attention. Witches were credited with a power to assume animal form and with possessing spirit familiars. The familiar might take the form of any animal but was most likely to appear as a dog, a cat, or a toad. Some familiars had no counterpart in natural history; one was described as having "paws like a bear but in bulk not fully as big as a coney." The ambiguity of such creatures was taken as evidence of their supernatural qualities. As Hopkins, the celebrated seventeenth century witchfinder, remarked, "No mortal alone could have invented them."

But my purpose has been to pose questions rather than to offer explanations. The particular diagrams which I have presented may not be the most useful ones, but at least I have established that the English language classification of familiar animals is by no means a simple matter; it is not just a list of names, but a complex pattern of identifications subtly discriminated not only in kind but in psychological tone. Our linguistic treatment of these categories reflects taboo or ritual value, but these are simply portmanteau terms which cover a complex of feeling and attitude, a sense perhaps that aggression, as manifested either in sex or in killing, is somehow a disturbance of the natural order of things, a kind of necessary impiety.

A Non-European Example

If this kind of analysis were applicable only to the categories of the English language it would amount to no more than a parlor game. Scientifically speaking, the analysis is interesting only in so far as it opens up the possibility that other languages analyzed according to similar procedures might yield comparable patterns. A demonstration on these lines is not easy: one needs to know a language very well indeed before one can play a game of this kind. Nevertheless it is worth trying.

Kachin is a Tibeto-Burman language spoken by hill tribesmen in Northeast Burma. Since it is grammatically and syntactically wholly unlike any Indo-European language it should provide a good test case. At one time I spoke the language fluently though I cannot do so now. I have a firsthand anthropological understanding of Kachin customary behaviors.

Kachin is essentially a monosyllabic language in which discrimination is achieved by varying the 'prefixes' of words rather than by tonal variation, though, as in other Tibeto-Burman languages, tones play their part. It follows that homonyms are very common in this language, and the art of punning and *double entente* is a highly developed cultural feature. A special form of lovers' poetry (*nchyun ga*) depends on this fact. A single brief example will suffice as illustration:

Jan du	gawng lawng	sharat a lo
At sunset	the clapper of the cattle bell	swings back and forth.
Mai bawt	gawng nu	sharat a lo*

The (buffalo's) short tail and the base of the bell   are wagged.

Nothing could be more superficially 'innocent' than this romantic image of dusk and cattle bells. But the poem takes on a very different appearance once it is realized that *jan du* (the sun sets) also means 'the girl comes (has an orgasm)' while *mai bawt* (the short tail) is a common euphemism for the human penis. The rest of the Freudian images can easily be worked out by the reader!

On the other hand, it cannot be said that the Kachin is at all 'foulmouthed.' Precisely because of his cultivated expertness at *double entente*, he can almost al-

---

* All Kachin linguistic usages cited here except the obscene connotation of *jan du* can be verified from O. Hanson (1906).

ways appear to be scrupulously polite. But verbal obscenities do exist, including what I have called animal abuse; the latter are mainly concentrated around the dog (*gwi*).

Kachins are a primitive people living in steep mountained forest country. Their diet consists mainly of rice and vegetables, but they keep cattle, pigs, and fowls. There are very few edible creatures which they will not eat, though they draw the line at dogs and rats and human beings. The domesticated animals are killed only in the context of a sacrificial ritual. The meat of such sacrifices is eaten by members of the attendant congregation, and sacrifices are frequent. Despite this frequency, the occasion of a sacrifice is a sacred occasion (*na*) and there is a sense in which all domestic animals are sacred.

Until very recently the Kachins had an institution of slavery. It is an indication of their attitude to animals rather than of their attitude to slaves that a slave was classed as a *yam*, a category which includes all domesticated animals. It is also relevant that the word *ni* meaning near also means tame.

The linguistic correlates of all this are not simple. In general, everything that has a place in ritual occasions falls into the wide category WU (U) meaning pollution. This has sundry subcategories:

(a) birds
(b) various species of bamboo
(c) creatures classed as *nga*—mainly fish and cattle
(d) creatures classed as *wa*—mainly human beings and pigs.

Ignoring the human beings and the bamboo, this is a category of polluted foods, i.e., foods which may properly be eaten only in the context of sacrifice. It contrasts with ordinary clean food and meat (*shat, shan*). Other creatures such as dog (*gwi*) and rat (*yu*) may sometimes be offered in sacrifice, but these would not be eaten except as part of some special magical performance. I have arranged these and other terms (Table 3) on a scale of social distance comparable to that shown for English language categories in Table 1. The parallels are very striking. Let us consider the items in this table reading from left to right, that is to say, from very close to very far.

The closest creatures are the dog and the rat. Both are inedible and heavily loaded with taboo. To call a man a dog is an obscenity; *yu* (rat) also means witchcraft. In some contexts it may also mean affinal relative on the wife's or mother's side. For a variety of structural reasons which I have described in other publications, a Kachin's feelings toward these *mayu ni* are ordinarily highly ambivalent. My wife's mother, a strongly incestuous category, is *ni*, which we have already seen also means very near, and tame.

The domesticated creatures that are edible if sacrificed have been considered already. These 'farm' creatures are much more closely identified with the self than the corresponding English categories. They are as human as slaves; they all live in the same house as their owners. The term *wa* (pig) also means man, father, tooth. It is veritably a part of 'me'!

In the English schema I suggested that field (game)

Table 3
KACHIN CATEGORIES OF FAMILIAR ANIMALS (for comparison with bottom three lines of Table 1)

	HOUSE (inedible)	FARM (edible if sacrificed)	FOREST (edible, no rules)	REMOTE (inedible)
	SELF-dog-rat	pig-cattle	small deer – large deer	elephant-tiger
			(near) (far)	
	gwi yu	wu / wa nga	hkyi tsu shan shat	gwi raw
Alternative English meanings of Kachin animal names in line above	(witch)		(feces) (ghost) (meat) (food)	(monster)

animals have the same structural position, in terms of social distance, as the category of potential wives. In the Kachin case the category of animals comparable to English game are the forest animals hunted for meat. They live in the forest (*nam*). Now the Kachin have a prescriptive rule of marriage which requires a man to marry a girl of a certain category; this category is also *nam*. But in other respects the Kachin case is the inverse of the English situation. An Englishman has free choice in obtaining a wife, but he must go further afield than a first cousin; on the other hand he hunts his game according to precise rules. In contrast the Kachin has his category of possible wives defined in advance and, as first preference, should choose a particular first cousin (the mother's brother's daughter). But he is subject to no rules when he hunts in the forest.

The creatures of the forest which are thus obtained for meat by hunting are mainly deer of various sizes. The smaller ones are found close to the village. Like the English rabbit these are regarded as vermin as well as game, since they raid the rice fields. The larger deer are found in the deep forest. There are in all four categories of deer: *hkyi* and *tsu* are both small species living close in, *shan* and *shat* are large creatures living far out. All these words have homonym meanings: *hkyi:* feces, filth; *tsu:* a disembodied human spirit, ghost; *shan:* ordinary (clean) meat food; *shat:* ordinary (clean) food of any kind.

Thus the pattern is quite consistent. The more remote animals are the more edible, and the homonym meanings of the associated words become less taboo loaded as the social distance is increased.

However, the over-all situation is not quite so simple. Monkeys of many kinds abound. They are sometimes eaten, occasionally tamed as pets, and their blood is credited with magical aphrodisiac qualities. They seem to be thought of as wild animals rather abnormally close to man, like the little deer *tsu*. A monkey is *woi*, a term which also means grandmother. The status of squirrels is very similar. The squirrel figures prominently in Kachin mythology, since it was the death of a squirrel that led man to become mortal. Squirrels are hunted and eaten, but again the attitude is ambiguous. Squirrels are *mai* (tails), but *mai* as we have already seen means a human penis.

Moreover, as remoteness is increased, we finally reach, as in English, a category of unknown and therefore inedible creatures, and the pattern is then reversed. There are two great beasts of the forest which the ordinary Kachin knows about but seldom sees. The first is the elephant, called *magwi* but also *gwi*. Since *gwi* is a dog this may seem odd, but the usage is very similar to that by which the English call the male fox a dog. The other is the tiger (*sharaw, raw*) which stands as the prototype for all fabulous monsters. *Numraw*, literally woman tiger, is a creature which figures prominently in Kachin mythology; she (?) has many attributes of the Sphinx in the Oedipus story, an all-devouring horror of uncertain sex, half man, half beast.*

---

* This greatly simplifies a very complex mythological category. The *numraw* (also *maraw*) are 'luck' deities, vaguely comparable to the

This over-all pattern, as displayed in Table 3, is certainly not identical to that found in English, but it is clearly very much the same kind of pattern, and the resemblances seem too close to be the product of either mere accident, as that phrase would ordinarily be understood, or the obsessional prejudices of myself as investigator. I suggest that the correspondences are at least sufficient to justify further comparative studies. On the other hand, I readily agree that it is easy to be over-persuaded by such evidence, especially when dealing with a language such as Kachin where the incidence of homonyms is very high.

In writing of English I suggested that there was a correspondence between the sequence of sex relationships: sister (incest); cousin (premarital relations possible, no marriage); neighbor (marriage possible); stranger (marriage impossible); and the sequence of 'edibility relationships' displayed in Table 1. How far does this apply for Kachin? How does one make the comparison? The difficulty is that Kachin has a kinship system quite different from that of English. True sisters are a strongly incestuous category, but remote classificatory clan sisters are persons with whom liaisons are possible but marriage is not. Elder sister is *na* and younger sister is *nau*. The homonyms are *na*, a sacred holiday, an occasion on which a ritual sacrifice is made; *nau*, a sacred dance occurring on *na* occasions to the accompaniment of sacrifice. This of course fits very

furies (erinyes) of Greek mythology. The *numraw* are not always female nor always of one kind. *Baren numraw* lives in the water and seems to be thought of as some kind of alligator, *wa numraw* is presumably a wild boar, and so on.

nicely with my thesis, for Table 3 can now be translated into human as opposed to animal relationships (in Table 4) thus:

Table 4
KACHIN CATEGORIES OF HUMAN RELATIONSHIPS

	incest	no marriage, illicit relations	marriage	remote nonrelative
SELF	NI	NA/NAU	NAM	RAW*
	mother-in-law	'sister'	marriageable cross-cousin	
	near	sacred occasion	forest	forest fire
	(inedible)	(edible if sacrificed)	(edible)	(inedible)

* There are two relevant homonyms of *raw* = tiger. *Raw* as a verb means cease to be related; it applies in particular when two affinally related groups cease to recognize their relationship. *Raw* also means forest fire. It is thus the dangerous aspect of the forest, where *nam* is friendly.

Perhaps all this is too good to be true, but I think that it deserves further investigation.

Those who wish to take my argument seriously might well consider its relevance to C. Lévi-Strauss's most remarkable book *La pensée sauvage* (1962). Though fascinated by that work I have also felt that some dimension to the argument is missing. We need to consider not merely that things in the world can be classified as sacred and not sacred, but also as more sacred and less sacred. So also in social classifications it is not sufficient to have a discrimination me/it, we/they; we also need a graduated scale close/far, more like me/less like me. If this essay is found to have a permanent value it will be because it represents an expansion of Lévi-Strauss's thesis in the direction I have indicated.

REFERENCES

Hanson, O. *A dictionary of the Kachin language.* Rangoon, 1906.

Lévi-Strauss, C. *La pensée sauvage.* Paris: Plon, 1962.

Partridge, E. *A dictionary of slang and unconventional English.* 3rd edition. London: Routledge, 1949.

Postman, L. The present status of interference theory. In Charles N. Cofer (Editor), *Verbal learning and verbal behavior.* New York: McGraw-Hill, 1961. Pp. 152-196.

Wentworth, H., and Flexner, S. B. *Dictionary of American slang.* New York: Crowell, 1961.

ERIC H. LENNEBERG*

A Biological Perspective of Language

The Relevance of Biology

At first it may seem as if biology had little to add to our knowledge of speech and language beyond the general and somewhat vague comparison of human communication with animal communication. I would like here to raise the question of whether there might not be biological endowments in man that make the human form of communication uniquely possible for our species.

The chief reasons for suspecting such specific biological propensities for our ability to acquire language are these:

1. *Anatomic and physiologic correlates.* There is increasing evidence that verbal behavior is related to a great number of morphological and functional speciali-

* Harvard University and Children's Medical Center.

Grateful acknowledgment is made for support through grants M-5268 and M-2921 from the National Institute of Mental Health.

zations such as oropharyngeal morphology (DuBrul, 1958); cerebral dominance (Ajuriaguerra, 1957; Mountcastle, 1962); specialization of cerebrocortical topography; special coordination centers (or foci) for motor speech; specialized temporal pattern perception; special respiratory adjustment and tolerance for prolonged speech activities; and a long list of sensory and cognitive specializations prerequisite for language perception.*

2. *Developmental schedule.* The onset of speech is an extremely regular phenomenon, appearing at a certain time in the child's physical development and following a fixed sequence of events, as if all children followed the same general "strategy" from the time they begin to the period at which they have mastered the art of speaking (Lenneberg, 1964; Morley, 1957; Weir, 1962). The first things that are learned are principles— not items: principles of categorization and pattern perception. The first words refer to classes, not unique objects or events. The sounds of language and the configuration of words are at once perceived and reproduced according to principles; they are patterns in time, and they never function as randomly strung up items. From the beginning, very general principles of semantics and syntax are manifest. Even if the maturational scale as a whole is distorted through retarding disease, the order of developmental milestones, including onset of speech, remains invariable (Lenneberg, Nichols, and Rosenberger, 1964). Onset and accomplishment of language

---

* More detailed treatment of this and the following point may be found in my forthcoming book, *The Biological Foundation of Language.*

learning do not seem to be affected by cultural or linguistic variations.

3. *Difficulty in suppressing language.* The ability to learn language is so deeply rooted in man that children learn it even in the face of dramatic handicaps. Congenital blindness has no obvious effect on word acquisition even though there is only a small fraction of words whose referents can be defined tactually. Congenital deafness has a devastating effect on the vocal facilitation for speech, yet presentation of written material enables the child to acquire language through a graphic medium without undue difficulties. Children suffering from gross and criminal parental neglect, or who have parents who have no spoken language whatever, as in the case of adult congenitally deaf parents, may nevertheless learn to speak with only a minimal delay, if any, according to research now in progress.

4. *Language cannot be taught.* There is no evidence that any nonhuman form has the capacity to acquire even the most primitive stages of language development. The vocalization skills and the behavioral responses to verbal commands that we find in a few species can be shown to bear merely a superficial resemblance to human verbal behavior. In each case it can be demonstrated that their behavior is based on fundamentally different principles from those in humans. The difference is not merely a quantitative one but apparently a qualitative one (Lenneberg, 1962b). No one has demonstrated that a subhuman form can acquire the principles of speech perception in terms of phonemic analysis, of understanding the syntactic structure of a sentence, or

of imparting the total semantic domain of any word, be it concrete or abstract.

5. *Language universals.* Although language families are so different, one from the other, that we cannot find any historical connection between them, every language, without exception, is based on the same *universal principles* of semantics, syntax, and phonology. All languages have words for relations, objects, feelings, and qualities, and the semantic differences between these denotata are minimal from a biological point of view. According to a number of modern grammarians (Chomsky, 1957; Greenberg, 1963; Hartmann, 1961; Hjelmslev, 1953) working quite independently of each other, syntax of every language shows some basic, formal properties, or, in other words, is always of a peculiar algebraic type. Phonologically, all languages are based on a common principle of phonematization even though there are phonemic divergences.

Language universals are the more remarkable as the speakers live in vastly different types of cultures ranging from an essentially neolithic type to the highly complex cultural systems of Western civilization. Further, language and its complexity is independent of racial variation. It is an axiom in linguistics that any human being can learn any language in the world. Thus, even though there are differences in physical structure, the basic skills for the acquisition of language are as universal as bipedal gait.*

---

* In an earlier paper (Lenneberg, 1961) I have defended the claim that universal features of language cannot be said to be either the most efficient or the most useful solution to acoustic communication except in a trivial sense: i.e., most useful for an organism that has the biological characteristics of man alone.

Owing to these considerations, it becomes plausible to hypothesize that language is a species-specific trait, based on a variety of biologically given mechanisms. Our task for the future is to discover and describe these mechanisms in greater detail than has been attempted so far.

This formulation poses three major problems which I shall now attempt to deal with:

1. Is uniqueness of behavior or form acceptable in the light of evolution?

2. Is there evidence for a genetic basis of language propensity?

3. Is language propensity a simple consequence of a general increase in "intellectual capacity," or must we assume some "language-specific" correlates?

Uniqueness of Species Characteristics

The discovery of a unique behavioral trait in a species need not mystify us, first, because we have been made aware by ethologists that speciation affects not only anatomy but also behavior, and that there are countless species with unique behavior patterns, and second, because uniqueness is to be expected from the evolutionary process itself.

There are two main processes in evolution: (1) clado-genesis, i.e., the process of branching out into newer and newer species; and (2) anagenesis or phyletic evolution, i.e., the process by which an entire species gradually undergoes change over time. If a given species fails to split up into isolated populations for a long period of time (or if only one of the newly resulting species survives), an animal with relatively unique traits will emerge. If the species has undergone anagenetic evolution, it will further deepen the gap between itself and its next of kin. According to Dobzhansky (1962), man's recent history is marked primarily by anagenesis; extinction of more closely related species has also taken place, as shown in Figure 1.

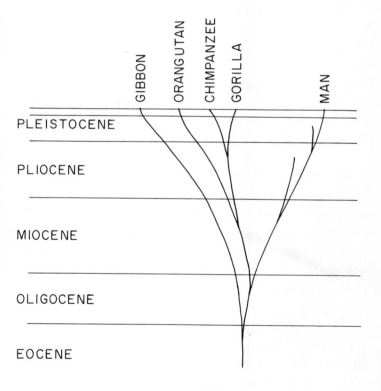

Fig. 1. Schema of the evolution of the Hominoidea.

The fact that man communicates with man is not a unique zoological phenomenon. Most animals have inter- and intraspecies communication systems, and among mammals there is usually vocal communication. However, the behavioral traits of animal communication cannot be ordered like a genetic tree and the phylogenetic relations among vertebrates, derived from comparative morphology, are not reflected in the taxonomy of their communication behavior. Many species have evolved highly specialized communication systems, such as the honeybee, many bird species, and dolphins. Neither these systems nor a dog's response to human commands represent primitive stages of human communication. Nor is there evidence that the communication of monkeys and apes constitutes a gradual approximation toward language. The empirically determined primitive beginnings of language in man (in the 18-months-old infant or in feeble-minded individuals) are behaviorally very different from the signals that animals emit for each other. Many animal communication systems are probably evolutionary offshoots, as is man's, and cross-species comparisons must be carried out with great caution.

Genetic Foundations

The genetic foundation of many types of behavior is widely recognized today (Fuller and Thompson, 1960; Hall, 1951). It is not assumed, however, that specific behavioral traits are directly produced by definite genes, but merely that propensities for certain behavior are inherited. This may be through changes in sensitivity thresholds or inherited perceptual, motor, or cognitive skills, such as changes in memory capacity (Rensch, 1954). Nevertheless, a unique or species-specific configuration of thresholds and skills may result through inherited propensities which make specific behavior uniquely possible. It is generally agreed that genes always affect a number of characters; this phenomenon is called *pleiotropism*. Pleiotropism is due to intramolecular rearrangements and may have in its wake disarrangements in the balance and harmony of embryological processes, particularly differentiation rates of tissues and growth gradients within the body. It is important to remember here that the developmental process is the unfolding of a continuously and precariously balanced affair where every single event is intimately related to a number of other events. Therefore, it is likely that genes often act on more than one property without interfering at the same time with the balance in other parts of the system. According to this view (Caspari, 1958), it is surprising that genetic changes are possible that are confined, phenotypically, to relatively circumscribed phenomena or, to put it differently, that, despite the frequent small changes that occur in the genotype, many characteristics of a species remain so completely stable.

Caspari explains the resistance of many characteristics to genetic change by postulating a gradient of "protection" against pleiotropic action. Thus, certain traits may be better established or more deeply rooted than others. Those that are well established tend to remain unaffected, even if genetic change has brought about thorough transfiguration of form and function in an individual. If, on the other hand, a given trait is not well protected, it is liable to change whenever there is any genetic disturbance interfering with the original state of balance. This is called polygenic inheritance, i.e., many different gene actions are capable of bringing about a given condition. Fertility is an example of polygenic inheritance in that it is very easily altered; most mutations are likely to affect it.

How do these concepts apply to language? The familial occurrence of language disabilities has been observed since the beginning of medicine. In recent years many reliable and careful studies have been published (Drew, 1956; Eustis, 1947; Gallagher, 1950; Hallgren, 1950; Luchsinger, 1959; Orton, 1930; Pfaendler, 1960), and the entire literature has been reviewed by Brewer (1963). On the basis of a carefully controlled and objective investigation of an entire family with congenital language disability (Fig. 2), Brewer concludes

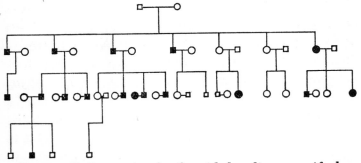

Fig. 2. Pedigree of a family with hereditary specific language disability. Circles are females; squares are males. Presence of trait is shown as solid symbols (Brewer, 1963).

that "specific language disability is a dominant, sex-influenced, or partially sex-linked trait with almost complete penetrance." In cases such as Brewer's there is never a total absence of language but merely a combination of certain deficits, including markedly delayed onset of speech, poor articulation persisting into the teens, poorly established hand preference, marked reading difficulties, either complete inability or marked difficulty for acquisition of second languages. Intelligence is usually not affected.

More direct evidence for the genetic basis of language comes from the work of Moorhead, Mellman, and Wenar (1961) who have made chromosome counts of a family in which a mother (Fig. 3) and four of her five children had a chromosomal abnormality associated with varying degrees of mental retardation and a striking failure of speech development. The father and a fifth sibling had a normal chromosome picture and were not affected behaviorally. Unfortunately, chromosome studies are too recent a development to have produced a large literature as yet. But it may be expected that in at least some families with specific language disability chromosome studies will eventually become available.

An important question that arises, especially from the Moorhead et al. study, is whether *any* chromosome abnormality is likely to lower intelligence and interfere with language. This is definitely not so. Some chromosome abnormalities are associated with somatic deficits without affecting intelligence, and other chromosome abnormalities affect intelligence but not necessarily language.

Although we have postulated that the propensity for language is the consequence of a pleiotropic effect, there is good reason to believe that the relevant genes are

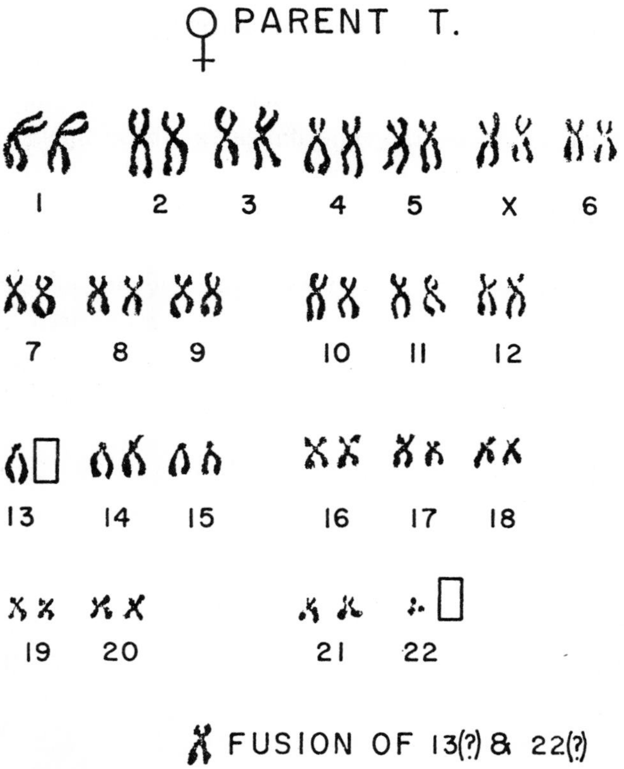

♀ PARENT T.

Fig. 3. Abnormal chromosome picture of woman with low intelligence and disproportionately poor speech and language. She gave birth to four children with similar chromosomal and clinical abnormalities. There is an unmatched chromosome which is interpreted as a fusion of missing chromosomes 13 and 22. Approximate enlargement 1200 ×. (Redrawn from Moorhead et al., 1961.)

well "protected" from the pleiotropic effect of other
genes; the propensity for language remains stable in
the presence of a great variety of clearly genetic alterations. We have mentioned that the morphological diversi-
fication of the races does not affect it. Nor is it affected
by the many traits that are apparently due to defects
in genes and that are inherited in Mendelian fashion,
such as hemophilia, Friedreich's ataxia, Huntington's
chorea, etc. Thus the inheritance for the propensity of
language deficits is not polygenic.

On the other hand, there is an inherited error of
metabolism producing a disease known as histidinemia
which has in its wake a very high incidence of specific
disturbance of language development in children, often
without affecting their intelligence or other behavioral
traits (Ghadimi, Partington, and Hunter, 1961, 1962;
Auerbach et al., 1962).

This is the extent of our evidence to date. It poses
the interesting question whether proof of language disturbance on a genetic basis is also evidence for the
genetic basis of language *ability*. Perhaps so, but more
work will have to be done before we can be relatively
certain. In any event, evolution and genetics appear
to be relevant to the general study of verbal behavior.

General or Specific Capacity

Nothing is gained by labeling the propensity for
language as *biological* unless we can use this insight
for new research directions—unless more specific correlates can be uncovered. At the present time we are

merely able to pinpoint certain biological problems and thereby to reopen some questions about language that were falsely thought to have been answered. For instance, it is often assumed that the propensity for language is simply a reflection of man's great non-specific intelligence. And as evidence for a "phylogenetic increase in intelligence," man's brain-weight/body-weight ratio is cited with the implication that the relative increase in neurons has made a certain level of intellect possible for language development. Both of these assumptions run into serious difficulties.

The definition and measurement of intelligence is difficult enough in our own species. When it comes to comparing different species, it is no longer permissible to talk about intelligence as if it were a single, clear-cut property that can be measured by a single objective instrument so as to yield quantities that are commensurable across species. Attempts have been made to compare across species such functions as memory span (Rensch, 1954), perceptual processes (Teuber, 1960), problem solving (Köhler, 1925), and others. In most of these instances, tasks are administered that are relatively easy for humans and more difficult for animals. On the other hand, tasks have been described in which various animals respond more quickly, with greater accuracy and, in a sense, more efficiently. Thus comparative psychology shows man to have a different mentation from other species and, obviously, a greater capacity to do things human. But we do not have objective and biologically meaningful proof that all mammals are endowed with a homogeneous and nonspecific amount of intelligence and that this amount increases with phylogenetic proximity to man.

Even if species could be compared in terms of general (surplus) intelligence and man could be shown to possess more of this quantity than any other creature, we still could not be certain that his ability for language is the result of, say, general inventiveness. Might it not be possible that language ability—instead of being the consequence of intelligence—is its cause? This has indeed been suggested by such thinkers as Hamann, Herder, W. v. Humboldt, Cassirer, and implied by Hughlings Jackson, Wundt, Whorf, Penfield, and many others before and since them. This proposition, which has been criticized for a number of reasons (Black, 1959; Feuer, 1953; Greenberg, 1954; Lenneberg, 1953, 1954, 1962a; Révész, 1954), is important in one respect: it suggests that language might be of greater biological antiquity than the peculiar intellective processes of recent man. Nevertheless, I do not advocate the notion that language is the cause of intelligence because there is no way of verifying this hypothesis. Instead, I would like to propose a *tertium quid*, namely, that the ability to acquire language is a biological development that is relatively independent of that elusive property called intelligence. I see evidence for this view in the fact that children acquire language at a time when their power of reasoning is still poorly developed and that the ability to learn to understand and speak has a low correlation with measured IQ in man. Let me elaborate on this latter point.

In a recent study Lenneberg, Nichols, and Rosenberger (1964) studied the language development of 84 feeble-minded children raised by their own parents in a normal home environment. The basic results are represented diagrammatically in Fig. 4. IQ figures, as measured by standard instruments, deteriorate with chronological age in the mentally retarded, even though there is objective growth in mental age up to the early teens, after which time mental development is arrested.

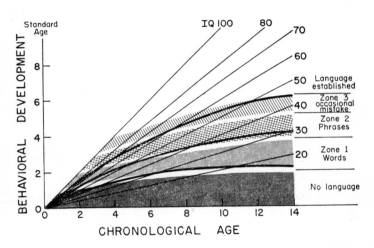

Fig. 4. Relationship between speech development and IQ. The curved lines show empirically determined "decay rates" of IQ in the mentally retarded. The shadings indicate language development. An individual whose IQ at a given age falls into the dark area at the bottom has no language. If he falls into the lighter areas, he is in one of three stages of language development and will develop further until his early teens, his progress depending upon both his IQ and his age. If he falls into the white area above, he is in full command of language. After age 12 to 13 speech development "freezes." (Data based on a follow-up study of 61 mongoloids and 23 children with other types of retarding disease.)

Language begins in the same manner in retardates as in the normal population. We found that it is impossible to train a child with, say, mongolism to parrot a complicated sentence if he has not yet learned the underlying principles of *syntax*. However, the general principle underlying *naming* is grasped at once and immediately generalized. Naming behavior may be observed even in low-grade idiots; only individuals so retarded as to be deficient in stance, gait, and bowel control fail to attain this lowest stage of language acquisition. Incidentally, it is interesting to note that generalization of naming is beyond the capacity of gorilla and chimpanzee.* Children whose IQ is 50 at age 12 and about 30 at age 20 are completely in possession of language though their articulation may be poor and an occasional grammatical mistake may occur.

Thus, grossly defective intelligence need not implicate language; nor does the *absence* of language necessarily lower cognitive skills. For instance, congenitally deaf children have in many parts of the world virtually no language or speech before they receive instruction in school. When these preschoolers are given nonverbal tests of concept formation they score as high as their age peers who hear (Furth, 1961; Rosenstein, 1960; Oléron, 1957). From these examples it appears that language and intelligence are to some extent at least independent traits. In order to prove their complete in-

---

* Viki, the chimpanzee raised by the Hayeses, could whisper "cup" when presented with a certain object by the Hayeses; but Mrs. Hayes describes how situation-bound the animal's naming behavior was. Room, time of day, examiner and acquaintance with object were all factors influencing the ability to understand and name correctly.

dependence it would be necessary to show that there are congenitally aphasic children whose nonverbal intelligence is unimpaired and who are also free from psychiatric disease. Many authorities believe that these cases exist, though in my experience I have not had occasion to examine such a patient. I have, however, studied one child (Lenneberg, 1962b) who had a congenital disability for articulation, who could not utter any intelligible word, but who did acquire the ability to understand language. Many other similar cases are familiar to me, constituting evidence that there is at least a highly particularly motor skill in man which may be selectively impaired by both discrete lesions and inherited defect.

Let us now return to man's brain-weight/body-weight ratio. Because of our difficulty in defining the phenomenon of intelligence zoologically, we shall circumvent the problem of the relationship of brain size and intellective power. Let us ask directly whether a large brain is the morphological prerequisite for language learning. Would it be possible to learn to understand or to speak a natural language such as English with a brain the size of some nonspeaking animal? The answer is *yes* but only if the individual is of the species *Homo sapiens*. This may sound like a contradiction in terms. Yet there is a clinical condition, first described by the German pathologist Virchow and named by him *nanocephalic dwarfism* (bird-headed dwarfs in the English-speaking world) in which man appears reduced to fairy-tale size. Seckel (1960) has recently described two such dwarfs and has reviewed the scientific literature on thirteen others. He ascribes the condition to a single-locus recessive gene for dwarfish stature without affecting endocrine organs and function. Adult individuals attain a maximum height of 3 feet, and about half of the described patients stand not much higher than $2\frac{1}{2}$ feet at adult age; the shortest adult mentioned measured 23 inches.

Nanocephalic dwarfs differ from other dwarfs in that they preserve the skeletal proportions of normal adults, as illustrated in Figure 5; the fully mature have a brain-body weight ratio well within the limits of a young teenager. Yet their head circumference and estimated

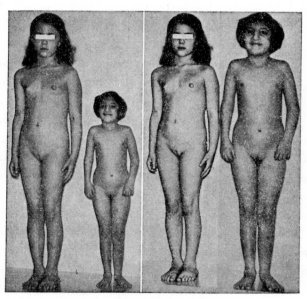

Fig. 5. Left: Nanocephalic dwarf next to normal girl of same age (9 years); right: the dwarf's photograph enlarged to show that bodily proportions are roughly similar to those of the normally developing girl (from Seckel, 1960; reprinted with the permission of S. Karger AG, Basel/New York).

brain weight barely exceed those of a newborn infant, as shown in Figure 6. On microscopic examination these brains have an unremarkable histological appearance;

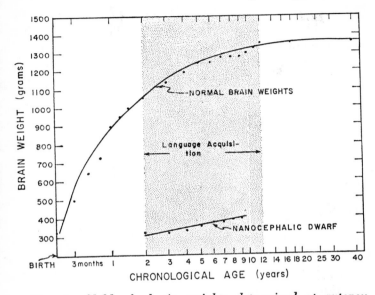

Fig. 6. Children's brain weights determined at autopsy plotted as a function of chronological age (based on data by Coppoletta and Wolbach, 1932). Bottom plot: various estimated weights based on repeated measurements of head circumference of patient shown in Fig. 5. The extrapolations were made by comparing autopsied children's head circumference with their brain weight.

both the size of individual nerve cells and the density of their distribution is within normal limits. Therefore we do not have here miniatured adult brains, but brains that differ very substantially from those of normal adults in the absolute number of cells. Intellectually, these dwarfs for the most part show some retardation,

often not surpassing a mental age level of 5 to 6 years.
All of them acquire the rudiments of language, including speaking and understanding, and the majority mas-
ter the verbal skills at least as well as a normal 5-year-
old child. From Table I it is apparent that neither the
absolute nor relative weights of brains and bodies reveal
the nature of the relationship between speech and its
neurological correlates. Apparently the ability to speak

Table 1

*BRAIN WEIGHTS AND BODY WEIGHTS OF
JUVENILE AND ADULT HOMINOIDEA*

	Age	Speech Faculty	Body Weight (Kg)	Brain Weight (Kg)	Ratio
Man (m)	2½	beginning	13½	1.100	12.3
Man (m)	13½	yes	45	1.350	35
Man (m)	18	yes	64	1.350	47
Man (dwarf)	12	yes	13½	.400[a]	34
Chimpanzee (m)	3	no	13½	.400[b]	34
Chimpanzee (f)	adult	no	47	.450[b]	104
Rhesus	adult	no	3½	.090[c]	40

[a] Estimate based on Seckel (1960).
[b] Estimate based on Schultz (1941).
[c] Estimate based on Kroeber (1948).

is not dependent upon nonspecific increase in cell number or anything as general as brain-weight/body-weight
ratios. Instead of postulating a quantitative parameter
as the critical variable for the ability to acquire language, we should look toward much more specific modes
of internal organization of neurophysiological processes.
At present we do not know what they might be. But
man's developmental and maturational history suggests
that growth processes and functional lateralization are
involved (Lenneberg, in press), the physical nature of
which remains to be discovered.

Conclusion

In the first part of this presentation I have argued that species-specific peculiarities are to be expected from the evolutionary processes themselves. Therefore, language specialization need not mystify us. In the second part I have tried to show that the basis for language capacity might well be transmitted genetically. In the last section I have rejected the notion that man's ability to speak is due to such general properties as an increase in intelligence or a relative increase in the weight of his brain. It seems, rather, as if language is due to as yet unknown species-specific biological capacities.

In conclusion I wish to emphasize that all these considerations serve to establish an hypothesis and to stimulate new directions for research on the nature of man. However, the facts presented do not constitute a theory. Let us hope they will lead to one in the future.

REFERENCES

Ajuriaguerra, J. de. Language et dominance cerebrale. *J. franç. d'Oto-Rhino-Laryngol.*, 1957, **6**, 489-499.

Auerbach, V., Digeorge, A., Baldridge, R., Tourtellotte, C., and Brigham, M. Histidinemia: A deficiency in histidase resulting in the urinary excretion of histidine and of imidazolepyruvic acid. *J. Pediatr.*, 1962, **60**, 487-497.

Black, M. Linguistic relativity: The views of Benjamin Lee Whorf. *Phil. Rev.*, 1959, **68**, 228-238.

Brewer, W. F. Specific language disability: Review of the literature and a family study. Honors thesis, Harvard University, 1963.

Caspari, E. Genetic basis of behavior. In A. Roe and G. G. Simpson (Editors), *Behavior and evolution*. New Haven: Yale University Press, 1958.

Chomsky, N. *Syntactic structures*. The Hague: Mouton, 1957.

Coppoletta, J. M., and Wolbach, S. B. Body length and organ weights of infants and children. *Amer. J. Pathol.*, 1932, **9**, 55-70.

Dobzhansky, T. *Mankind evolving*. New Haven: Yale University Press, 1962.

Drew, A. L. A neurological appraisal of familial congenital word-blindness. *Brain*, 1956, **79**, 440-460.

DuBrul, E. L. *Evolution of the speech apparatus*. Springfield, Ill.: Thomas, 1958.

Eustis, R. S. The primary etiology of the specific language disabilities. *J. Pediatr.*, 1947, **31**, 448-455.

Feuer, L. S. Sociological aspects of the relation between language and psychology. *Phil. Sci.*, 1953, **20**, 85-100.

Fuller, J. L., and Thompson, W. R. *Behavior genetics*. New York: John Wiley, 1960.

Furth, H. The influence of language on the development of concept formation in deaf children. *J. abnorm. soc. Psychol.*, 1961, **63**, 386-389.

Gallagher, J. R. Specific language disability: A cause for scholastic failure. *New Engl. J. Med.*, 1950, **242**, 436-440.

Ghadimi, H., Partington, M., and Hunter, A. A familial disturbance of histidine metabolism. *New Engl. J. Med.*, 1961, **265**, 221-224.

Ghadimi, J. R., Partington, M., and Hunter, A. Inborn error of histidine metabolism. *Pediatrics*, 1962, **29**, 714-728.

Greenberg, J. H. Concerning influences from linguistic to nonlinguistic data. In Harry Hoijer (Editor), *Language in culture*. Chicago: University of Chicago Press, 1954.

Greenberg, J. H. (Editor). *Universals of language*. Cambridge, Mass.: M.I.T. Press, 1963.

Hall, C. S. The genetics of behavior. In S. S. Stevens (Editor), *Handbook of experimental psychology*. New York: John Wiley, 1951.

Hallgren, B. Specific dyslexia (congenital word-blindness). *Acta psychiatr. neurol. scand.*, 1950, Suppl. **65**.

Hartmann, P. Allgemeinste Strukturgesetze. In *Sprache und Grammatik*. The Hague: Mouton, 1961.

Hjelmslev, L. *Prolegomena to a theory of language.* Indiana University Publications in Anthropology and Linguistics, Memoir 7. Baltimore: Waverly Press, 1953.

Köhler, W. *The mentality of apes.* New York: Harcourt, Brace, 1925.

Kroeber, A. L. Anthropology. New York: Harcourt, Brace, 1948.

Lenneberg, E. Cognition in ethnolinguistics. *Language,* 1953, **29**, 463-471.

Lenneberg, E. A note on Cassirer's *Philosophy of Language. Phil. phenomenol. Res.*, 1954, **15**, 512-522.

Lenneberg, E. Language, evolution and purposive behavior. In S. Diamond (Editor), *Culture in history.* New York: Columbia University Press, 1961.

Lenneberg, E. The relationship of language to the formation of concepts. *Synthèse,* 1962a, **14**, No. 2/3, 103-109.

Lenneberg, E. Understanding language without ability to speak: A case report. *J. abnorm. soc. Psychol.*, 1962b, **65**, 419-425.

Lenneberg, E. Speech as a motor skill with special reference to non-aphasic disorders. In U. Bellugi and R. Brown (Editors), The acquisition of language. *Child Developm. Monogr.*, 1964, **29**, 115-126.

Lenneberg, E. Speech development: Its anatomical and physiological concomitants. In V. E. Hall (Editor), *Speech, language and communication. Brain and Behavior* (in press).

Lenneberg, E. H., Nichols, I. A., and Rosenberger, E. F. Primitive stages of language development in mongolism. *Proc. Assoc. Res. nerv. ment. Disease,* 1964, **42**, 119-137.

Luchsinger, R. Die Vererbung von Sprach und Stimmstoerungen. *Folia phoniatr.,* 1959, **11**, 7-64.

Moorhead, P. S., Mellman, W. J., and Wenar, C. A familial chromosome translocation associated with speech and mental retardation. *Amer. J. hum. Genet.*, 1961, **13**, 32-46.

Morley, M. *The development and disorders of speech in child-hood*. Baltimore: William & Wilkins, 1957.

Mountcastle, V. B. (Editor). *Interhemispheric relations and cerebral dominance*. Baltimore: Johns Hopkins University Press, 1962.

Oléron, P. *Recherches sur le developpement mental des sourdes-muets*. Paris: Centre National de la Recherche Scientifique, 1957.

Orton, S. T. Familial occurrence of disorders in the acquisition of language. *Eugenics*, 1930, **3**, No. 4, 140-147.

Pfaendler, U. Les vices de la parole dans l'optique du géné-ticien. *Akt. Probl. der Phoniatr. und Logopaed.*, 1960, **1**, 35-40.

Rensch, B. *Neuere Probleme der Abstammungslehre*. Stuttgart, 1954.

Révész, G. Denken und Sprechen. In G. Révész (Editor), *Thinking and speaking: A symposium*. Amsterdam: North Holland, 1954.

Rosenstein, J. Cognitive abilities of deaf children. *J. Speech Hearing Res.*, 1960, **3**, 108-119.

Schultz, A. H. The relative size of the cranial capacity in primates. *Amer. J. Anthropol.*, 1941, **28**, 273-287.

Seckel, H. P. G. *Birdheaded dwarfs: Studies in developmental anthropology including human proportions*. Springfield, Ill.: Thomas, 1960.

Teuber, H.-L. Perception. In J. Field, H. W. Magoun, and V. E. Hall (Editors), *Handbook of physiology*. Section 1: Neurophysiology, Vol. III. Washington, D. C.: American Physiological Society, 1960.

Weir, R. H. *Language in the crib*. The Hague: Mouton, 1962.

GEORGE A. MILLER*

Language and Psychology

Only a man brave to the point of foolhardiness could begin a topic such as mine without an apology. The vast and variegated realms of language and psychology cannot be covered in a few general remarks, however wise they may be, and no one—with the possible exception of a physicist I know who likes to lecture on The Universe and Other Things—no one could seriously hope even to state, much less solve, all the problems that they pose. Obviously, I cannot address the larger issues that my title suggests. I can only hope to share with you some of the particular topics that have caught my eye, and try to communicate to you my personal interest in them.

It would be valuable, however, if I could begin by offering you a cognitive map of the domain that is the general setting for my particular interests—partly to illustrate how much I will not be able to discuss, and

* Harvard University. This paper was supported by funds granted to Harvard University, Center for Cognitive Studies, by the Department of Defense, Advanced Research Projects Agency, Contract SD-187.

partly to keep us both from getting lost. There are, of course, a variety of such maps that we might adopt. Each discipline that touches on the relation of thought and language seems to have surveyed the area and erected signposts for its own convenience.

The traditional map of language and psychology, of course, derives from philosophical psychology and is based on the three-way distinction among affection, conation, and cognition. When applied to language— as by Karl Bühler (1933), for example—this scheme usually emphasizes the expressive, persuasive, and descriptive functions that language can play in our thinking and in our daily affairs. If these three are not sufficiently discriminating, we could accept the three additional functions of language—the poetic, the phatic, and the metalingual functions—suggested more recently by the linguist Roman Jakobson (1960). Or if a classification by functions is inappropriate, we might become more analytic and arrange our thoughts according to the idealized components of a communication system— the source, the encoder, the channel and its interferences, the decoder, and the receiver—after the fashion of Claude Shannon (1948) and the communication engineers. Or, from the same perspective, we might try to use the classification of processes into message, code, signal, and noise. These are neutral kinds of maps, about equally useful to linguists and psychologists. Or if we were desperate we might even borrow the classification used so widely by students of aphasia—receptive, amnesic, and expressive—as a way of organizing our discussion.

All of these schemes have their own special advantages, but none of them pleases everybody. Let me say quite clearly that I am not fond of any of them—or of any of the dozen other classification schemes that I have heard proposed. They remind me too much of the old classifications into fire, air, earth, and water, or into blood, phlegm, choler, and black choler that once played such an important role in physics and biology. But although I dislike them, at the present time such rude classifications are all we have to indicate which region of this vast subject we are talking about at any particular moment.

And so I shall adopt one of them, not because I like it but because I do not know how else to proceed. I shall adopt a kind of logico-philosophical frame of reference—in the spirit of Charles Morris (1938)—and divide the study of signs and symbols into three parts: syntactics, semantics, and pragmatics.

Roughly speaking, syntactic studies are concerned with the relation of signs to signs. Semantics deals with the relation of signs to their meanings. And pragmatics is concerned with the relation of signs to the people who use them. The general effect of this scheme is to divide the field into problems of structure, of comprehension, and of belief, so that, if you accept it as a way of thinking about the psychological processes involved in linguistic knowledge and behavior, it leads you into a kind of hierarchy of processes: at the lowest level it is necessary to understand the syntactic structure; then it becomes possible to understand its semantic content; and at the top, after both structural analysis and semantic comprehension are achieved, pragmatic acceptance or rejection, belief or disbelief, is possible.

In defense of such an orientation, I can say only that it seems to correspond roughly with the order in which the study of language has progressed. At the present time linguists and logicians have a rather deep understanding of syntax and have formalized their discoveries in axiomatic systems. As yet the semantic aspects have not been clearly defined, so that nothing very interesting can presently be said at a theoretical level, but one gets a feeling from much current work by philosophers, linguists, and ethnographers that the general shape a semantic theory must assume is slowly emerging. Pragmatics, however, is still the wastebasket into which all miscellaneous and confusing problems are put, a category that by definition defies definition.

It is not difficult for a psychologist to find objections to such a scheme, for in any strict interpretation of it the psychologist's interest must be classified as pragmatic. He becomes interested only when people are explicitly involved, and he tries to deal with the ways in which people acquire, understand, and exploit the properties of linguistic systems. But from what I have just said about the formless nature of pragmatic studies of language, this is not a very pleasant place to find oneself. From the psychologist's point of view, therefore, the principal function of this approach is to separate his pragmatic interests from the more formalized studies of syntactics and semantics—to eliminate certain areas of work as clearly not his responsibility. He should know them, of course, but he need not create them. And so we need not look at everything in linguistics or everything in psychology but can focus more directly on the pragmatic area of overlap between them.

With this orientation, therefore, one is led to what I consider an extremely important distinction, namely, the distinction between theories of language and theories of language users (Miller and Chomsky, 1963). Let me try to elaborate this distinction in terms of logic, rather than in terms of grammar, for in logic the situation is analogous but better defined. A logician is interested in discovering the rules for valid inference, but whether people actually use those rules or not does not concern him. The student of thinking, on the other hand, knows all too well that people are illogical, and that the processes that go on when they attempt to use logic have little resemblance to the axiomatic system of Russell and Whitehead. In this domain, therefore, we have little difficulty in accepting a distinction between the theory of logic and the theory of logic users. My argument is simply that this distinction is just as valid and as valuable in the study of natural languages as it is in the study of the artificial notations of logic and mathematics.

In all candor, however, I must admit that most of my linguistic friends resist this distinction with passion and tenacity. They argue that a description of a natural language that does not also describe the verbal behavior of the people who speak that language would be an empty exercise, of little use to anyone. They reject any attempt to banish them off into a formal wasteland of logical and mathematical formulae, where inferences can never be tested against reality, but only checked for internal consistency and simplicity. However, the distinction I wish to draw between theories of language and theories of language users need not, and probably should not, be taken as the boundary between linguistics and psychology. There is, as I have already indicated, a large area of overlap between psychology and linguistics, a pragmatic area where both must work shoulder to shoulder—the linguist trying to test his formulation of the rules of the language, the psychologist trying to test his formulation of the psychological processes whereby the language user succeeds or fails in obeying those rules. How a linguist works with his informants in the field and how a psychologist works with his experimental subjects in the laboratory are not independent and unrelated; each science can learn much from studying the techniques and procedures of the other.

Having now narrowed my topic to the pragmatic study of language, and having defined it as the attempt to construct theories of language users, let me next remark that one of the first and most pressing tasks that faces us in constructing such theories is to understand how the person deals with the syntactic and semantic aspects of language, with structure and meaning. Having just thrown these topics out on their formal ear, I must now drag them back in on their empirical foundations.

It would be simpler, of course, if we did not need pragmatic theories of syntax and semantics, but I do not see how to escape them. Every time I have tried to explore the psychological reality of syntactic and semantic rules, I have found them to have large and important effects on the behavior of my subjects. I have not enough time, nor you enough patience, for a detailed description of all the various ways we have explored this question, but let me describe one study we have done, just by way of illustration.

In this particular study, we tried to vary both the syntactic and the semantic features of the materials we presented to our subjects. We did this in the following way. First, we constructed a set of five five-word sentences, all having the same syntactic structure. For example, *Furry wildcats fight furious battles, Respectable jewelers give accurate appraisals, Lighted cigarettes create smoky fumes, Gallant gentlemen save distressed damsels,* and *Soapy detergents dissolve greasy stains.* Let me call these the normal grammatical sentences. We then constructed a new set of five sentences, derived from and having the same syntactic structure as the original set, by simply selecting the first word from the first sentence, the second word from the second, the third from the third, and so on. In this example, the result was *Furry jewelers create distressed stains, Respectable cigarettes save greasy battles, Lighted gentlemen dissolve furious appraisals. Gallant detergents fight accurate fumes,* and *Soapy wildcats give smoky damsels.* Let me call these the semantically anomalous sentences. Next we constructed some sentence anagrams out of the original set of sentences. For example, we took *Furry wildcats fight furious battles* and scrambled the order of the words to give *Furry fight furious wildcats battles,* and *Respectable jewelers give accurate appraisals* was turned into *Jewelers respectable apprai-*

sals accurate give, and so forth. In these, which I shall call anagrammatic strings, the words all can be assimilated to a rather small semantic field, but the syntactic structure is destroyed. And finally we took the semantically anomalous sentences and scrambled them, thus producing *Furry create distressed jewelers stains, Cigarettes respectable battles greasy save,* and so forth, where both the semantic and the syntactic aspects are violated and we are left with nothing but haphazard strings of words.

Armed with these four types of materials, we moved into the psychological laboratory. In our first experiments (Miller and Isard, 1963) we asked people to listen to these materials spoken in the presence of a masking noise, and to repeat into a recording device exactly what they thought they heard. In a later experiment (Marks and Miller, 1964) we asked people to memorize the sentences by the method of free recall. In both the perceptual and the learning experiments the over-all results were the same. The normal grammatical sentences were the easiest to hear and to remember, the semantically anomalous sentences and the anagrammatic strings were intermediate and about equally difficult, and the haphazard strings of words were by far the most difficult of all.

From an intuitive, common-sense point of view, I suppose there is nothing very surprising about this result. The subjects came to our laboratory equipped with well-learned syntactic and semantic habits. When the materials were normal grammatical sentences, they could transfer these skills to the experimental task. And as we made their linguistic habits progressively less applicable, less transfer was possible, and the task became progressively more difficult. All of which is true enough.

There is another point of view, however, from which these results can seem rather discouraging. If you are trying to construct a theory of speech perception or of verbal learning, you might hope to be able to solve all your problems at the level of phonetics or at the level of words and nonsense syllables. These experiments with sentences, however, show clearly that the problems are much more complex than that, and that any complete theories of speech perception or verbal learning will have to cope with the syntactic and semantic rules that a person uses when he listens or learns.

This is but one of several lines of evidence I could marshall to try to persuade you that our theories of the language user must include a description of how he learns and uses the syntactic and semantic rules of his language. But perhaps I need not labor the point any further. Unless you happen to be advocating some rival hypothesis, I suspect you will accept my statement as at least obvious, if not banal.

Which leaves us with an interesting question of sufficient generality that I would like to bring it up and make it more explicit. The syntax and semantics of a language are generally stated in the form of a system of rules—grammatical and lexical rules. The language user knows those rules, since he can, within limits that are of considerable psychological interest, follow them in generating and understanding grammatical utterances. But what is the scientific status of a rule as an explanatory concept in psychology? It is not a law, for it can be violated, and often is. Ordinarily, one would like to define a rule as an explicit statement, couched in some formal or informal notation, that specifies the appropriate actions to take under certain well-defined circumstances. But this conception of a rule as an explicit statement is ill-suited to the situation in psycholinguistics, for it is generally the case that people who can follow the rules with amazing skill are often completely unable to provide any explicit statement of the rules they are following. If people know the rules, therefore, they must know them implicitly. The only way we know they know the rules is by inference from the fact that, under certain carefully specified circumstances, their behavior conforms to them, and from the fact that they can recognize what it means to make a mistake.

I believe that an implicit rule must be called a habit. But this term stirs up as many problems as it solves. Most of the work that psychologists have done with habits has investigated very simple habits that can be described most simply and directly in terms of the stimulus and response elements of the situation. But this is extremely difficult, if not impossible, when we are describing linguistic habits, for the variety of stimulus-response associations that are available when one knows a language is many orders of magnitude greater than he would have time to learn in a finite childhood.

Indeed, the magnitude of the learning task and the speed with which children accomplish it seem to me to be impressive arguments that children must be naturally endowed with a remarkable predisposition for language learning. I will not push this point, for fear of invading topics that Drs. Carmichael and Lenneberg have already discussed, but I mention it because the term habit has acquired such an empiricist coloring in modern psychology. I believe, however, that when we talk about linguistic rules as habits, we should remember that these are habits that human beings are uniquely prepared to acquire—that there is, so to speak, a large nativistic component in our ability and proclivity for acquiring habitual linguistic rules.

People are capable of dealing—and do deal constantly—with linguistic events that are completely new to them. The important point here is that syntactic and semantic habits must have a character that linguists call *productive*. It is their productivity that distinguishes our linguistic rules from our other, simpler habits. On the basis of a finite exposure to grammatical and meaningful utterances, we are able to deal with an infinite variety of different and novel utterances. When this ability has been encountered in simpler situations, psychologists have frequently dealt with it in terms of stimulus and response generalization. But there is good reason to believe that the kind of productive generalization that goes on when we use language is of a completely different order of complexity. A description of habit that is adequate to deal with productive as well as with reproductive habits will be much more complicated than most of the theories currently under investigation in our psychological laboratories.

I would like to emphasize that productivity is a pervasive characteristic of language. It is generally accepted, I believe, that syntactic habits must have a productive character, because the supply of different sentences, unlike the supply of words, is unlimited. But the same kind of problem emerges at the semantic level, too. There have, of course, been numerous attempts to deal with the referential properties of individual words by likening them to conditioned reflexes or other simple stimulus-response associations. I believe, however, that a careful consideration of the semantic relation between a word and its referent (when it has one) will convince most people that it should be described as a rule, not as some simpler and more automatic kind of habit. The challenging problem, however, does not appear at the level of individual words, but at the level of sentences, where these words combine according to higher-order semantic rules, at present but poorly understood, to yield the meaning we assign to the total sentence (Katz and Fodor, 1963). Somehow we are able to combine the meanings to obtain an understanding of the meaning of the sentence, and we are able to do this for sentences that are completely new to us and that express ideas we have never heard or thought of before. I see no alternative but to conclude that semantic habits must also be productive.

Of course, our pragmatic task of constructing a theory of the language user will not be complete when we have managed to account for the productivity of our syntactic and semantic habits. There will still remain features of language that are purely pragmatic, and many of these have their productive aspects, too. I think it is fair to characterize the main concern of pragmatics as the construction of a psycholinguistic theory of belief —where I would define belief systems quite broadly, of course, to include any type of acceptance or commitment that could lead to action. To say that we believe a proposition implies that, under appropriate circumstances, we would take action or make decisions based on it. In its most general form, therefore, belief is what gives language its powerful control over our behavior. Here again we encounter an unlimited variety of combinations of beliefs that must somehow be related to one another in a systematic fashion. But this is such an ill-formulated topic that I hesitate to pursue it further.

In general, therefore, our task of constructing a theory of language users has been stated in terms of the description of productive syntactic, semantic, and pragmatic habits. I find it difficult to develop this argument, however, without becoming involved in some particular set of habits that I can use to illustrate more concretely what I have in mind and what kind of research is possible within such a framework.

When one begins to describe linguistic habits, he finds almost immediately that they come in all shapes and sizes, and the first step must be to isolate one or more of them that can then be controlled and subjected to experimental investigation. It would be simpler, of course, if we could conduct one ultimate, crucial experiment that would establish some sovereign principle from which all the petty details could then be deduced. But the details included in the intersection of language and psychology are not likely to submit so easily; we are condemned to chip away at this mountain of complexity one small puzzle at a time.

There are a variety of psycholinguistic phenomena that have been investigated to the point where they could serve as useful examples, but I must choose a single one. Somewhat arbitrarily, I have decided to tell you what I know (or think I know) about the various kinds of linguistic habits that control our use of negation. Negation is a powerful concept, and there is much that no one understands about its psycholinguistic basis, but let me try to summarize what seems to be our current state of knowledge about it.

Psycholinguists have known for many years—perhaps it was Smoke (1932) who first stated it explicitly —that negative instances of any given concept are more difficult for people to understand and use than are positive instances. This fact has been demonstrated under so many different circumstances that we can feel confident it is a fairly ubiquitous phenomenon—not something peculiar to Smoke's concept-formation task. Hovland and Weiss (1953) were even able to demonstrate the superiority of positive instances when the informational value of both positive and negative instances had been carefully controlled in advance.

I did not become personally interested in this problem until I read reports of some experiments by Peter Wason (1959, 1961), which suggested to me that perhaps a grammatical as well as logical difficulty was involved. In an ingenious series of experiments Wason was able to show that it takes longer to evaluate negative sentences than positive, and that, under certain conditions, the affirmative-negative difference for that task is more important than the difference between true and false sentences. That is to say, for the evaluation task, syntactic form was more important than semantic content.

At the time I read these studies I had been working with Mrs. Kathryn Ojemann McKean on the possibility of measuring the times required to perform various grammatical transformations. We had been using a sentence-matching technique (Miller, 1962); we informed the subject of the grammatical transformation he was to make, then gave him a sentence to transform, and measured the time it took him to transform it and find the transformed version in a list of alternative sentences. By taking differences between the times measured in this way and the times measured when no transformation —merely search—was required, we were able to estimate the transformation times for negative and for passive transformations and for both together. We had found that the negative transformation takes about 1 second, the passive takes about $1\frac{1}{2}$ seconds, and the two together take as much time as the sum of the times taken individually. (On the basis of more recent work, using better experimental techniques, we now believe that those estimates are too long, but the general pattern of relations among them has persisted in further experiments.)

The significant point, however, was that the time differences observed in Wason's experiments might have been attributable, at least in part, to the time required to perform the grammatical transformations from negative to affirmative statements. The implicit assumption here is that, before a subject could respond to a negative sentence, he had to transform it into an affirmative statement and change its truth value, and that the additional time required for negative sentences was occupied with performing these grammatical and logical transformations.

If this conjecture were true, therefore, a simple way to test it would be to inquire whether, under the conditions used by Wason, passive sentences also took longer to evaluate, since one might expect that a similar kind of grammatical unraveling would be involved in processing them. When Dr. Lee E. McMahon (1963) expressed interest in this problem, I encouraged him to explore it; I can now report to you the general results he obtained.

McMahon found that it took his subjects about 0.1 second longer to evaluate passive than active sentences, and about 0.4 second longer to evaluate negative than affirmative sentences, and that—as we had found in our clumsier sentence-matching studies—the extra time required to evaluate negative-passive sentences could be predicted directly by summing the times required for each transformation alone. He performed this experiment in three different ways and this general conclusion appeared under all conditions. And so it seemed that there might be some substance to the hypothesis that at least part of the difficulty in using negatively phrased information is attributable to the difficulty in unscrambling its grammatical form.

But could all of the difficulty be attributed to grammar? McMahon did not find that it took as long as one would expect from our sentence-matching tasks to evaluate the truth or falsity of passive sentences. Wason, who was visiting at the Harvard Center for Cognitive Studies while McMahon was conducting these experiments, was convinced that it could not all be explained by syntax. And so he undertook another experiment to prove his point. As many people have remarked, negative statements are ordinarily used for the correction of plausible errors. You do not say *It is not raining* unless there is some plausible reason for your listener to think that it might have been raining. Following this line of thought, Wason designed an experiment to see if it took longer to complete negative sentences about unexceptional facts than about exceptional facts. Or, more precisely, he predicted that the difference between the times required to complete affirmative and negative sentences about exceptional situations would be smaller than the difference between them when they described unexceptional situations. And his data confirmed his prediction. Apparently it is much easier, and certainly more natural, in describing a pattern of one blue and seven red dots, to say that *one dot is not red* than to say that *seven dots are not blue*. Since I know of nothing in the theory of grammar that would lead one to predict such an outcome, I am forced to agree with Wason that there is more to this matter than syntax alone can account for.

I believe that this little tale of experimental psycholinguistics can be used to illustrate how psychologists are beginning to work at the syntactic, semantic, and pragmatic levels of language. The studies by Mrs. Mc-Kean and myself were directed at a purely syntactic question: could we measure the times required to make grammatical transformations? Since Wason's and Mc-Mahon's experiments required the subject to understand sentences and judge their truth value, they moved the problem on to the level of semantic analysis. And finally, Wason's demonstration that negative sentences about exceptional situations are easier to produce than one would expect on syntactic or semantic grounds seems to introduce a pragmatic factor, for the negative is commonly used to correct a prior belief in its affirmative counterpart. Each level of investigation enriched our understanding of the linguistic habits governing our use of negation in English.

Negation, of course, represents only one small suburb in the vast metropolis of our linguistic habits, and even there we still have much to learn before our theories can be complete. Other suburbs have been invaded, however, and progress, though slow, is encouraging. It is now possible to look forward to the time when we will have conquered, if not the whole city, then at least some of the major regions within it.

Then, and only then, I believe, will we begin to understand what it is that a person has learned when he learns to speak a natural language.

REFERENCES

Bühler, K. Die Axiomatik der Sprachwissenschaft. *Kant-Studien*, 1933, **38**, 19-90.

Hovland, C. I., and Weiss, W. Transmission of information

concerning concepts through positive and negative instances. *J. exp. Psychol.*, 1953, **45**, 175-182.

Jakobson, R. Linguistics and poetics. In T. A. Sebeok (Editor), *Style in language.* Cambridge, Mass.: Technology Press, 1960. Pp. 350-377.

Katz, J. J., and Fodor, J. A. The structure of a semantic theory. *Language,* 1963, **39**, 170-210.

Marks, L., and Miller, G. A. The role of semantic and syntactic constraints in the memorization of English sentences. *J. verb. Learn. verb. Behav.*, 1964, **3**, 1-5.

McMahon, L. E. Grammatical analysis as a part of understanding a sentence. Ph.D. thesis, Harvard University, 1963.

Miller, G. A. Some psychological studies of grammar. *Amer. Psychologist,* 1962, **17**, 748-762.

Miller, G. A., and Chomsky, N. Finitary models of language users. In R. D. Luce, R. R. Bush, and E. Galanter (Editors), *Handbook of mathematical psychology.* New York: Wiley, 1963. Vol. 2, pp. 419-491.

Miller, G. A., and Isard, S. Some perceptual consequences of linguistic rules. *J. verb. Learn. verb. Behav.*, 1963, **2**, 217-228.

Morris, C. W. Foundations of the theory of signs. In O. Neurath, R. Carnap, and C. W. Morris (Editors), *International encyclopedia of unified science.* Chicago: University of Chicago Press, 1938. Pp. 77-137.

Shannon, C. E. A mathematical theory of communication. *Bell Sys. tech. J.*, 1948, **27**, 379-423.

Smoke, K. L. An objective study of concept formation. *Psychol. Monogr.*, 1932, **42**, No. 191.

Wason, P. C. The processing of positive and negative information. *Quart. J. exp. Psychol.*, 1959, **11**, 92-107.

Wason, P. C. Response to affirmative and negative binary statements. *Brit. J. Psychol.*, 1961, **52**, 133-142.

FRIEDA GOLDMAN-EISLER*

Discussion and Further Comments

I. Formal Discussion

I think it is fair to say that there is a disinclination in the ranks of our science to accept the proclivity of the human species for language as a special grace of nature, and this should not surprise us. At a time when English Lords put up a spirited fight to be allowed to shed their privilege and join the Commons, our need to embrace the animal world as peers if somewhat less developed seems only another facet of the "Zeitgeist." And the *tabula rasa* approach to propensities is more in keeping with it than the idea of innate endowment.

Nevertheless, the speakers in this symposium, having immersed themselves in the study of language phenomena and viewed them in a wide variety of fields, suggest that the facts do not support such attitudes; that, in the light of a growing understanding of what is involved when we use language, explanations based on S-R associations exclusively are no longer tenable.

The idea of a reduction of language and speech to

* University College, London.

a skill achieved through a conditioning process, in complexity but not in principle distinct from the one operative in animal training, has been examined by them in the light of knowledge drawn from the biological sciences on the one hand and modern linguistic analysis and anthropology on the other. The explanations advanced on this basis, by releasing the psychology of language from the constraints of reflex-arc theorizing, accommodate many more facts of linguistic behavior than could be accounted for within its limits.

This becomes evident if these facts of linguistic behavior are viewed in the light of the range of functions encompassed in the act of speaking: of the links it provides between physiological and logical operations, between the animal cry and symbolic expression, between the individual and society, and also of the fact that speech involves the use of organs whose primary task is to serve vital biological needs. We need only consider that articulate sound is produced through the combined activity of the respiratory tract, the pharynx, the tongue, the lips, the teeth, etc.—organs all of which have been developed during the course of evolution to serve the primitive functions of eating, breathing, and crying in emotion—while at the same time speech is not possible without the functioning of the highest levels and latest organs of the brain.

Dr. Carmichael, who is concerned with the facts of the law of development of this organic machinery and of the mechanisms of its inherent capacity, shows that before the skill of speaking can begin to be learned these mechanisms must be in working order.

I think we must be grateful to him for first clearing the deck for a better understanding of the difference between the languages serving communication between animals and human speech. Here the confusion has been great and has affected zoologists as well as psychologists. His clarification of the term "meaning," and the clear distinction he makes between the two ways in which it is used, concedes a limited use to the concept of meaning, in terms of strength of response, as a tool of one-way manipulation, but shows that meaning in fully developed human speech requires a mutual "understanding" and that this is its distinctive feature. Such a subjective term may be anathema to many of our colleagues, but those who enjoy the irony of facts will appreciate his report that recent extensive studies of chimpanzee communication in the wild support an earlier suggestion by Yerkes that, for all practical purposes of social life and organization, some primates are probably better served by *their* linguistic systems than man is by *his* language, and that in fact the only *raison d'être*, the only function, for the spoken language of man seems to be representation of ideas.

There is, it appears, no escaping either the connection of human speech with thinking or the dichotomy of speech between automatic vocalization and considered utterance or true, real, meaningful speech in Carmichael's terms. Or is there, at least as far as the dichotomy of speech is concerned?

Can this bipolarity of speech be bridged over when viewed in developmental terms? Carmichael speaks of tracing the "surely meaningful" to "surely nonmeaningful" sound production, and it seems that the fact of a differential rate in the maturation of the speech centers, with its production of a brain state manifesting itself as speech readiness, introduces the kind of additional information that can link discrete phenomena and show them to be continuous.

But this continuity has a three-dimensional configuration, as distinct from the linear continuity envisaged in S-R explanations. In other words, if the law of anticipatory function works, as Carmichael shows in the development of speech mechanisms, we can no longer act as if we were dealing with a skill built up unidirectionally in so many steps of reinforcement. The maturational sequence in the human infant's ability to use meaningful words, must be taken into account in any study of language growth. Carmichael shows a way by defining a specific area of research involving the study of cortical anatomy, histology, and physiology to be correlated with recorded word utterance. It is hard to see how the science of language (and of man) can fail to profit from this new opening.

Dr. Lenneberg makes the point by showing that there is no way of teaching an organism the principles of speech perception unless the organism brings to the learning situation a peculiar way of processing the incoming data. This will, I think, hardly be contended even by ardent S-R theorists, which may be a measure of progress in the sophistication on the subject. For we have only to think of how much work has gone into teaching apes to speak, to appreciate how persistent and determined the efforts were which went into denying hu-

man language the properties of uniqueness and irre-
ducibility.

Yet Lenneberg's elaboration that this way of processing data consists in the principles of grammar, universal
to all languages, manifest in semantics, syntax, and
phonology, and that in this respect human languages are
unique and language is a species-specific trait, a product
of genetics and evolution, takes us well into the center
of present-day argument in psycholinguistics. For the
controversy has moved on to the problem of the mechanism of speech production and is now being fought on
the issue of sequential vs. structure determination in
the generation of speech.

A further point made by Dr. Lenneberg that these
propensities seem to be extremely well protected in the
cell matter and that they are subject to less variation
or vicissitudes than nonspecific intelligence is crucial,
because he draws from this, together with other facts,
the conclusion that language and intelligence are, to
some extent at least, independent traits.

At some point, of course, nonspecific intelligence must
have its impact on linguistic behavior and vice versa—
and here we come to grips with the problem of the
speech-thought relationship. But if Lenneberg is right,
then at least we would know that there are two clearly
distinct and genetically separated propensities involved.
This is most important, for instance, in trying to understand what exactly has been the loss in aphasic disorders.

The understanding of the relationship and interaction
between linguistic capacities and nonspecific intelligence
is, of course, altogether of wide practical consequence.

The issue is complicated by additional cultural factors, for instance, as was recently shown in London (Bernstein, 1962) by class determination of capacities for verbal planning. The resultant of these forces seems to have a decisive influence on the educability of working-class children, which acts across the determination by nonspecific intelligence. The degree of verbal planning was measured in terms of hesitation pauses in spontaneous speech.

From my own investigations on hesitation pauses in spontaneous speech, I am led more and more to believe that there may be at work a factor of internal time, or a capacity for the delay of action, which determines the degree of the impact that nonspecific intelligence may have, or be allowed to have, on linguistic expression, particularly in respect of degree of planning. This must have biological as well as social roots.

Planning is an indispensable concept when it comes to trying to understand what is involved in manipulating syntactical skills for semantic ends. Professor Miller has, in his book on *Plans and the Structure of Behavior* (1960), defined a plan as "any hierarchical process in the organism that can control the order in which a sequence of operations is to be performed." This applies to all organized behavior, but in none are we in such a favored position to study this process as in human speech. In none are the steps by which the plan is executed so overt, so externalized by the nature of the phenomenon, and in none is this process so well regulated and subject to well-established plans, the grammatical rules, as in language behavior. These rules take a central position in the process of speech production, as Miller points out. They are generative of a range of possible choices of words, phrases, and meaning, and there is still a good amount of freedom within them; on the other hand, the application of particular rules, their juxtaposition, their coordination and subordination are subject to over-all planning, metaplans as Miller might say.

When we speak a language we usually, though not invariably, follow these rules, most language users not knowing, as Miller points out, that they are doing so, these rules being implicit and unstated for most speakers. I think it is Chomsky (1959) who makes the point that this process of behaving lawfully when the law is unknown can only mean that grammar is part of our behavior—that we are endowed with it—which again recalls Lenneberg's case for an inherent linguistic propensity.

Miller advances our thinking on the subject by making the connection between this process of behaving lawfully when the law is unknown and the characteristic of productivity that distinguishes our linguistic rules from other simpler habits, the capacity, that is, for generating an infinite variety of new linguistic combinations.

I think that by following this direction we may learn more about those activities of the brain which generate what, at the highest level, is described as ingenious, original, or novel. The series of experiments he cites which drew his attention to semantic productivity is in this direction and is an intriguing example of experimental psycholinguistics, showing how a semantic complication, an element of meaning generated in addition to grammatical operations, can be spotted simply because it takes more time.

The use of time as a measure of the number and complexity of operations, and the idea of the dual nature of speech which he conceives in terms of production and reproduction, leads me to my own experiments in which I studied the function of hesitation pauses in spontaneous speech.

These owe a great deal to Hughlings Jackson's thinking and his classical division of speech phenomena. The great virtue of Jackson's division is that its distinctive features are determined by the generating processes involved. His so-called "superior" speech is a voluntary act, an act of "propositionizing" (indicating that the unit of speech is the proposition, not the isolated word), which is being performed at the time of speaking. Such a speech is "newly organized" and fitted to the meaning intended. Hughlings Jackson classifies as "inferior" speech which he describes as "old" in the sense of being "well organized," familiar, consisting of learned sequences and ready-made phrases, and whose production was an automatic act. The distinctive feature is thus the novelty of the process, and this is in keeping with Miller's description of the property of "productivity" in speech as one that results in the utterance and understanding of an infinite variety of novel sentences whose meanings and syntax we have never encountered before.

The relationship between brain processes and speech situation is in Hughlings Jackson's system conceived to be a dynamic one. Any sequence of words could, according to this system, become inferior, i.e., automatic, once it was well learned. Vice versa, the "same" utterance which has become automatic by being often used would become once more "voluntary speech" if it were used on a new occasion. The criterion is thus psychological or neurophysiological, not linguistic.

Productivity becomes an event in the here and now of the speech act. In normal speech, we must think of it as embedded in a large mass of automatic verbal behavior—only in the aphasic the bipolarity of speech comes to the surface, and productivity is dissociated from habitual verbalization.

Normal speech might be viewed as a highly integrated blend of processes at both levels, an apparently linear phenomenon in which voluntary and automatic activities are closely interlaced, propositional construction alternating with the use of ready-made phrases, choice in fitting words to meaning with submission to the routine course and to the constraints of learned sequences: in short, where results of conditioning alternate with spontaneous creation.

Miller is dealing with this question of linear vs. the hierarchical structure-theory of speech generation by investigating the problem of grammatical rules, and by linking the objective linguistic product to the generating process.

II. An Experimental Approach to Psycholinguistic Problems

My own experiments approached the distinction between the two levels of speech generation as a problem of measurement, applied to spontaneous speech, such as we meet in conversations, discussions, undirected interviews, and verbal assignments that leave the subjects free in their choice of language. Such speech was chosen for study because here the speaker is thinking on his (or her) feet, is organizing speech on the spur of the moment, is improvising. The purpose of the experiments designed with this material was to see whether one might not be able to isolate, from the relatively orderly flow of spontaneous speech, elements that might prove to be indicative of the different levels of speech production, bringing into the open the dissociation that catastrophe may produce in the aphasic, by means of measurement.

The phenomenon which emerged as the most profitable to measure in this context was that of pausing which interrupts the flow of spontaneous speech. This we express as a ratio of the duration of pauses to the number of words in any utterance.

The measurement of hesitation pauses in large tracts of conversational speech of verbally competent adults reveals facts which in themselves throw light on the problems of speech generation.

There is the fact of discontinuity in the so-called flow of speech. In most cases speech comes in strings of words separated by pauses of varying duration.

The transposition of sound recordings into graphic form shown in Figure 1 illustrates this fact. These pauses are frequent as well as time consuming. Half of our

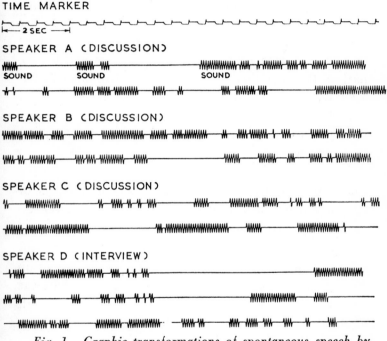

Fig. 1. Graphic transformations of spontaneous speech by four speakers. Each line represents a period of 10 seconds.

speech time seems to issue in phrases not longer than three words, and three quarters in phrases of fewer than five words at the most (Goldman-Eisler, 1961a). An average of 40 to 50 per cent of utterance time is occupied by pauses (Goldman-Eisler, 1961b). Evidently pausing is as much part of the act of speaking as the vocal utterance of words itself, which suggests that it is essential to the generation of spontaneous speech.

Another fact resulting from these measurements which is relevant here is that pausing is the main factor accounting for variation in the rate of speech production (i.e., output of speech syllables per time unit); the rate of articulation (i.e., of the vocal act of speaking) proved in comparison remarkably constant and has no part in the variations of speech rate (Goldman-Eisler, 1956). This is not altogether surprising if we consider that the vocal act of speaking is a highly skilled performance with the consequent narrow scope for variation that goes with such performances.

Pausing, on the other hand, with its extremely wide range of variation might well represent that aspect of speech which has little call on skill and which reflects the nonskill part of speech production.

One would therefore expect pausing to be the behavior concomitant of the productive processes in the brain concerned with verbal planning and selection, whereas continuous and rapid vocalization would be the result of practice and would occur when the gaps have been closed in the use of well-learned word sequences.

These conclusions I was able to confirm by showing that hesitation pauses precede a sudden increase of information, estimated in terms of transition probabilities (Goldman-Eisler, 1958a). Delay proved an important element in the production of information in speech, and fluent speech was shown to consist of habitual combinations of words such as are shared by the language community.

Beyond helping us to discriminate between the two kinds of speech—or rather between the relevant processes involved in their production—the procedure of estimating transition probabilities—Shannon's guessing game (Goldman-Eisler, 1958a)—revealed the insufficiency of linear explanation, according to which speech is a matter of mere associative linkage of elements in sequence, a left-to-right progression of word choices; for the estimates became more significant, and the relation between information and hesitancy reciprocal, only when the transition probabilities were derived from guesses in the reverse as well as the forward direction (Figure 2).

It then turned out that some of the words which were difficult to guess when guessing left to right were easy when going right to left, and vice versa; but only those words which guessers found difficult coming either way were preceded by pauses in the original utterances (these are the 17 out of 21 in the enclosure of Figure 3).

The fluency of the left-to-right progression of external speech is thus affected by the ties that link words not only to what preceded but also to what is yet to come. This can hardly be explained on the basis of purely associative linkage, without the assumption of a structural plan of some sort guiding the choice of words in verbal sequences.

A further, otherwise unintelligible, result also becomes plausible with the assumption of a syntactic-plus-semantic framework. In this experiment (Goldman-Eisler, 1958b) subjects were asked to read incomplete sentences and to fill the blanks with the words omitted;

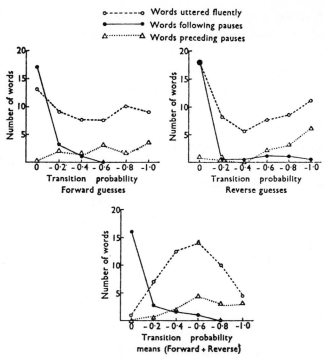

Fig. 2.   Frequency distributions of transition probabilities for words uttered fluently, words following pauses, and words preceding pauses based on forward guesses, reverse guesses, and averaged forward and reverse guesses.

they were asked to do this as they were going along reading the sentences; these sentences had been lifted from other subjects' recorded conversations, and their pauses had been measured. There were two conditions: in one, the blanks were substituted for words of high transition probability, in the other, for words of low transition probability. The delays in filling these blanks were significantly longer in the first condition. But cut-

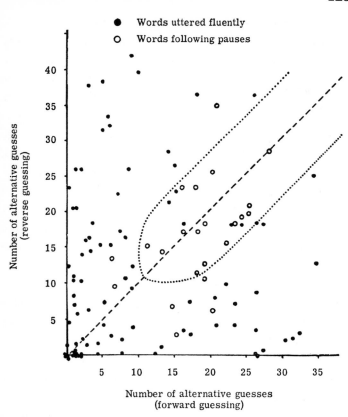

Fig. 3. Figure showing relation between forward and reverse guesses and position of alternatives guessed in respect of least square space. Abscissa shows alternative words guessed from left to right; ordinate from right to left.

ting across these conditions, these delays and the pauses of the original speakers were found to be proportional in length in those sentences in which the readers completed the blanks correctly (*P* less than .02). No such relation existed where they had failed.

In interpreting these results the following is to be considered: duplicating the original wording must surely imply that the reader is operating within the same context as the original speaker, that he is able to conjecture the original speaker's intention as far as meaning, as well as sentence structure, is concerned. One may perhaps think in terms of a tentative schema, an image guiding his guesses and facilitating his lexical decisions, this image being the link between the reader and the original speaker, a shared knowledge that determines the pausing of both of them alike. Where the reader was unable to make correct guesses, this link must have been missing. Without it, word choice, in accordance with sequential forces, seems to break down. The results of both experiments are incompatible with the assumption of statistical determination of speech as the only factor in its generation; in order to explain them we must postulate processes distinct from those that follow the principles of association by contiguity.

The assumption that hesitation pauses in speech are the delays due to processes taking place in the brain whenever speech ceases to be the automatic vocalization of learned sequences, whether occasioned by choice of an individual word, by construction of syntax, or by conception of content, led to a further experiment in which thought construction was made an indispensable and controlled part of a speaking process (Goldman-Eisler, 1961c).

New Yorker cartoons like the one in Figure 4 were shown, and subjects were asked to describe their story and then formulate their meaning, their point, in a con-

the cartoons. Sequential information is reorganized and recoded into the form of a general statement. Association by contiguity is transformed into association by similarity.

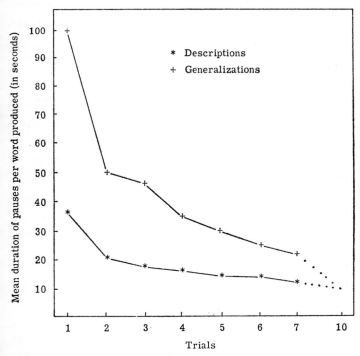

Fig. 5. Hesitancy at two levels of verbal planning and its decrease with repetition.

The results, given in Figure 5, showed that:

1. The amount of pausing when formulating the meaning of events, when recoding the description in general terms, was twice as much as when describing the events in their sequence.

2. Pausing also varied with the different degrees of spontaneity, as may be seen from the diagram. The sudden decline after the first trial and the gradual decrease of pausing in the subsequent repetitions indicate that the difference between spontaneity and reiteration, between production and reproduction, is a qualitative one.

We then estimated transition probabilities for the verbal material produced in this experiment (743 words and 43 sentences were involved—255 words and 19 sentences in the generalizations, and 479 words, 24 sentences, in the descriptions), playing the Shannon game in forward and reverse directions.

The sentences for descriptions and generalizations were then divided into two groups, those whose utterance was fluent and those whose utterance was preceded by a pause.

Table 1 shows their ratios of words of low to words

Table 1
RATIOS OF LOW (0 TO 0.2) TO HIGH (0.8 TO 1.0) TRANSITION PROBABILITIES

	Fluent Speech	Hesitant Speech	Total
Descriptions	1.57	3.00	1.85
Generalizations	4.89	9.50	5.73

of high transition probability: in low are included words of not more than $P = 0.2$, and in high, words of 0.8 to 1.0.

We can see that predicting words in sentences describing the cartoon stories was easier all round than predicting individual words in sentences used in the generalizations, i.e., when formulating their meaning. In the context of generalizing the guessers found more words difficult and less words easy to predict, even where the original speaker attained the same degree of fluency as in the descriptions. Although it discriminated significantly between fluent and hesitant words used in the descriptions ($X^2 = 6.5$, P less than .01), transition probability did not do so with the words used in the generalizations ($X^2 = 1.07$).

The implications of these facts seem again to be relevant to our problem of structure plus meaning, or syntactic plus semantic vs. linear determination. For it seems that where the operation required for the formulation of the speech content is more difficult, as it is when meaning is abstracted, the guessers' share of the information, of the context which determines the speaker's lexical choices, is reduced; or to put it differently, that at the level of generalizing from specific events, the speaker's choices were more individual, even where he was more fluent (which might occur after his semantic decision had been made), or that, at the level of recoding, a greater amount of information was the speaker's own, that this was a level of speech generation which was more private and subjective, and that the sequence had ceased to be a matter of common conditioning and learning. When linguistic communality is thus reduced, prediction according to sequential dependencies is less successful. As the speaker's task was to conceive a proposition of his own to fit the story, while at the same time giving it a more universal significance, the context from which the choice of his words would to a considerable degree stem was novel and of his own creation. Again the facts are fitted best with the assumption of a semantic plus grammatical determination, above and in addition to the sequential, statistical one.

REFERENCES

Bernstein, B. Linguistic codes, hesitation phenomena and intelligence. *Language and Speech,* 1962, **5**, Part 1, 31-46.

Chomsky, N. Review of B. F. Skinner, *Verbal behavior. Language,* 1959, **35**, 26-58.

Goldman-Eisler, F. The determinants of the rate of speech and their mutual relations. *J. psychosom. Res.,* 1956, **2**, 137-143.

Goldman-Eisler, F. Speech production and the predictability of words in context. *Quart. J. exp. Psychol.,* 1958a, **10**, 96-106.

Goldman-Eisler, F. The predictability of words in context and the length of pauses in speech. *Language and Speech,* 1958b, **1**, Part 3, 226-231.

Goldman-Eisler, F. Continuity of speech utterance, its determinants and its significance. *Language and Speech,* 1961a, **4**, Part 4, 220-231.

Goldman-Eisler, F. The distribution of pause durations in speech. *Language and Speech,* 1961b, **4**, Part 4, 232-237.

Goldman-Eisler, F. Hesitation and information in speech. In Colin Cherry (Editor), *Information theory.* London: Butterworths, 1961c.

Miller, G. A. *Plans and the structure of behavior.* New York: Holt, 1960.

ROGER BROWN AND URSULA BELLUGI*

Three Processes in the Child's Acquisition of Syntax

Some time in the second six months of life most children say a first intelligible word. A few months later most children are saying many words and some children go about the house all day long naming things (*table, doggie, ball,* etc.) and actions (*play, see, drop,* etc.) and an occasional quality (*blue, broke, bad,* etc.). At about 18 months children are likely to begin constructing two-word utterances; such a one, for instance, as *push car.*

A construction such as *push car* is not just two single-word utterances spoken in a certain order. As single-word utterances (they are sometimes called holophrases) both *push* and *car* would have primary stresses and terminal intonation contours. When they are two words programmed as a single utterance the primary

* Harvard University. This investigation was supported by Public Health Service Research Grant MH-7088 from the National Institute of Mental Health.

stress would fall on *car* and so would the highest level of pitch. *Push* would be subordinated to *car* by a lesser stress and a lower pitch; the unity of the whole would appear in the absence of a terminal contour between words and the presence of such a contour at the end of the full sequence.

By the age of 36 months some children are so advanced in the construction process as to produce all the major varieties of English simple sentences up to a length of 10 or 11 words. For several years we have been studying the development of English syntax, of the sentence-constructing process, in children between 18 and 36 months of age. Most recently we have made a longitudinal study of a boy and girl whom we shall call Adam and Eve. We began work with Adam and Eve in October 1962 when Adam was 27 months old and Eve 18 months old. The two children were selected from some 30 whom we considered. They were selected primarily because their speech was exceptionally intelligible and because they talked a lot. We wanted to make it as easy as possible to transcribe accurately large quantities of child speech. Adam and Eve are the children of highly educated parents, the fathers were graduate students at Harvard and the mothers are both college graduates. Both Adam and Eve were single children when we began the study. These facts must be remembered in generalizing the outcomes of the research.

Though Adam is 9 months older than Eve, his speech was only a little more advanced than hers in October 1962. The best single index of the level of speech development is the average length of utterance, and in

October 1962 Adam's average was 1.84 morphemes and Eve's was 1.40 morphemes. The two children stayed fairly close together in the year that followed; in the records for the 38th week Adam's average was 3.55 and Eve's, 3.27. The processes we shall describe appeared in both children.

Every second week we visited each child for at least 2 hours and made a tape recording of everything said by the child as well as of everything said to the child. The mother was always present and most of the speech to the child is hers. Both mother and child became very much accustomed to our presence and learned to continue their usual routine with us as the observers.

One of us always made a written transcription, on the scene, of the speech of mother and child with notes about important actions and objects of attention. From this transcription and the tape a final transcription was made, and these transcriptions constitute the primary data of the study. For many purposes we require a "distributional analysis" of the speech of the child. To this end the child's utterances in a given transcription were cross-classified and relisted under such headings as: "$A +$ noun"; "Noun $+$ verb"; "Verbs in the past"; "Utterances containing the pronoun *it*," and so forth. The categorized utterances expose the syntactic regularities of the child's speech.

Each week we met as a research seminar, with other students of the psychology of language,* to discuss the

* We are grateful for intellectual stimulation and lighthearted companionship to Jean Berko Gleason, Samuel Anderson, Colin Fraser, David McNeill, and Daniel Slobin.

state of the construction process in one or the other of the two children as of that date. In these discussions small experiments were often suggested, experiments that had to be done within a few days if they were to be informative. At one time, for instance, we were uncertain whether Adam understood the semantic difference between putting a noun in subject position and putting it in object position. Consequently one of us paid an extra visit to Adam equipped with some toys. "Adam," we said, "show us the duck pushing the boat." And when he had done so: "Now show us the boat pushing the duck."

Another week we noticed that Adam sometimes pluralized nouns when they should have been pluralized and sometimes did not. We wondered whether he could make grammatical judgments about the plural, whether he could distinguish a correct form from an incorrect form. "Adam," we asked, "which is right, 'two shoes' or 'two shoe'?" His answer on that occasion, produced with explosive enthusiasm, was: "Pop goes the weasel!" The two-year-old child does not make a perfectly docile experimental subject.

The dialogue between mother and child does not read like a transcribed dialogue between two adults. Table 1 offers a sample section from an early transcribed record. It has some interesting properties. The conversation is, in the first place, very much in the here and now. From the child there is no speech of the sort that Bloomfield called "displaced," speech about other times and other places. Adam's utterances in the early months were largely a coding of contemporaneous events and impulses. The mother's speech differs from the speech that adults use to one another in many ways. Her sentences are short and simple; for the most part they are the kinds of sentences that Adam will produce a year later.

Table 1
A SECTION FROM ADAM'S FIRST RECORD

Adam	Mother
See truck, Mommy.	
See truck.	
	Did you see the truck?
No I see truck.	
	No, you didn't see it?
	There goes one.
There go one.	
	Yes, there goes one.
See a truck.	
See truck, Mommy.	
See truck.	
Truck.	
Put truck, Mommy.	
	Put the truck where?
Put truck window.	
	I think that one's too large to go in the window.

Perhaps because they are short, the sentences of the mother are perfectly grammatical. The sentences adults use to one another, perhaps because they are longer and more complex, are very often not grammatical, not well formed. Here for instance is a rather representative example produced at a conference of psychologists and linguists: "As far as I know, no one yet has done the in a way obvious now and interesting problem of doing a in a sense a structural frequency study of the alternative syntactical in a given language, say, like English, the alternative possible structures, and how what their hierarchical probability of occurrence structure is" (Maclay and Osgood, 1959). It seems unlikely that a child could learn the patterns of English syntax from such speech. His introduction to English ordinarily comes in the form of a simplified, repetitive, and idealized dialect. It may be that such an introduction is necessary for the acquisition of syntax to be possible, but we do not know that.

In the course of the brief interchange of Table 1, Adam imitates his mother in saying: "There go one" immediately after she says "There goes one." The imitation is not perfect; Adam omits the inflection on the verb. His imitation is a reduction in that it omits something from the original. This kind of imitation with reduction is extremely common in the records of Adam and Eve, and it is the first process we shall discuss.

Imitation and Reduction

Table 2 presents some model sentences spoken by the mothers, together with the imitations produced by Adam and Eve. These utterances were selected from hundreds in the records to illustrate some general propositions. The first thing to notice is that the imitations preserve the word order of the model sentences. To be sure, words in the model are often missing from the imitation, but the words preserved are in the order of the original. This is a fact that is so familiar and somehow reasonable that we did not at once recognize it as an empirical outcome, rather than as a natural necessity. But of course it is not a necessity; the outcome could have been otherwise. For example, words could have been said back in the reverse of their original order, the most recent first. The preservation of order suggests that the model sentence is processed by the child as a total construction rather than as a list of words.

Table 2
SOME IMITATIONS PRODUCED BY ADAM AND EVE

Model Utterance	Child's Imitation
Tank car	*Tank car*
Wait a minute	*Wait a minute*
Daddy's brief case	*Daddy brief case*
Fraser will be unhappy	*Fraser unhappy*
He's going out	*He go out*
That's an old time train	*Old time train*
It's not the same dog as Pepper	*Dog Pepper*
No, you can't write on Mr. Cromer's shoe	*Write Cromer shoe*

In English the order of words in a sentence is an important grammatical signal. Order is used to distinguish among subject, direct object, and indirect object, and it is one of the marks of imperative and interrogative constructions. The fact that the child's first sentences preserve the word order of their models accounts in part for the ability of an adult to "understand" these sentences and so to feel that he is in communication with the child. It is conceivable that the child "intends" the meanings coded by his word orders and that, when he preserves the order of an adult sentence, he does so because he wants to say what the order says. It is also possible that he preserves word order just because his brain works that way and that he has no comprehension of the semantic contrasts involved. In some languages word order is not an important grammatical signal. In

Latin, for instance, "Agricola amat puellam" has the same meaning as "Puellam amat agricola" and subject-object relations are signalled by case endings. We would be interested to know whether children who are exposed to languages that do not utilize word order as a major syntactic signal preserve order as reliably as do children exposed to English.

The second thing to notice in Table 2 is that, when the models increase in length, there is not a corresponding increase in the imitation. The imitations stay in the range of 2 to 4 morphemes, which was the range characteristic of the children at this time. The children were operating under some constraint of length or span. This is not a limitation of vocabulary; the children knew hundreds of words. Neither is it a constraint of immediate memory. We infer this from the fact that the average length of utterances produced spontaneously, where immediate memory is not involved, is about the same as the average length of utterances produced as immediate imitations. The constraint is a limitation on the length of utterance the children are able to program or plan.* This kind of narrow-span limitation in children is characteristic of most or all of their intellectual operations. The limitation grows less restrictive with age, as a consequence, probably, of both neurological growth and practice, but of course it is never lifted altogether.

A constraint on length compels the imitating child to omit some words or morphemes from the mother's longer sentences. Which forms are retained and which

---

* See Brown and Fraser (1963) for additional evidence of the constraint on sentence length.

omitted? The selection is not random but highly systematic. Forms retained in the examples of Table 2 include: *Daddy, Fraser, Pepper,* and *Cromer*; *tank car, minute, brief case, train, dog,* and *shoe*; *wait, go,* and *write*; *unhappy* and *old time.* For the most part they are nouns, verbs, and adjectives, though there are exceptions, as witness the initial pronoun *He* and the preposition *out* and the indefinite article *a.* Forms omitted in the samples of Table 2 include: the possessive inflection -*'s,* the modal auxiliary *will,* the contraction of the auxiliary verb *is,* the progressive inflection -*ing,* the preposition *on,* the articles *the* and *an,* and the modal auxiliary *can.* It is possible to make a general characterization of the forms likely to be retained that distinguishes them as a total class from the forms likely to be omitted.

Forms likely to be retained are nouns and verbs and, less often, adjectives, and these are the three large and "open" parts of speech in English. The number of forms in any one of these parts of speech is extremely large and always growing. Words belonging to these classes are sometimes called "contentives" because they have semantic content. Forms likely to be omitted are inflections, auxiliary verbs, articles, prepositions, and conjunctions. These forms belong to syntactic classes that are small and closed. Any one class has few members, and new members are not readily added. The omitted forms are the ones that linguists sometimes call "functors," their grammatical *functions* being more obvious than their semantic content.

Why should young children omit functors and retain contentives? There is more than one plausible answer. Nouns, verbs, and adjectives are words that make reference. One can conceive of teaching the meanings of these words by speaking them, one at a time, and pointing at things or actions or qualities. And of course parents do exactly that. These are the kinds of words that children have been encouraged to practice speaking one at a time. The child arrives at the age of sentence construction with a stock of well-practiced nouns, verbs, and adjectives. Is it not likely then that this prior practice causes him to retain the contentives from model sentences too long to be reproduced in full, that the child imitates those forms in the speech he hears that are already well developed in him as individual habits? There is probably some truth in this explanation but it is not the only determinant since children will often select for retention contentives that are relatively unfamiliar to them.

We adults sometimes operate under a constraint on length, and the curious fact is that the English we produce in these circumstances bears a formal resemblance to the English produced by two-year-old children. When words cost money there is a premium on brevity or, to put it otherwise, a constraint on length. The result is "telegraphic" English, and telegraphic English is an English of nouns, verbs, and adjectives. One does not send a cable reading: "My car has broken down and I have lost my wallet; send money to me at the American Express in Paris" but rather "Car broken down; wallet lost; send money American Express Paris." The telegram omits *my, has, and, I, have, my, to, me, at, the, in.*

All of these are functors. We make the same kind of telegraphic reduction when time or fatigue constrains us to be brief, as witness any set of notes taken at a fast-moving lecture.

A telegraphic transformation of English generally communicates very well. It does so because it retains the high-information words and drops the low-information words. We are here using "information" in the sense of the mathematical theory of communication. The information carried by a word is inversely related to the chances of guessing it from context. From a given string of content words, missing functors can often be guessed, but the message, "my has and I have my to me at the in," will not serve to get money to Paris. Perhaps children are able to make a communication analysis of adult speech and so adapt in an optimal way to their limitation of span. There is, however, another way in which the adaptive outcome might be achieved.

If you say aloud the model sentences of Table 2 you will find that you place the heavier stresses, the primary and secondary stresses in the sentences, on contentives rather than on functors. In fact the heavier stresses fall, for the most part, on the words the child retains. We first realized that this was the case when we found that, in the transcribing of the tapes, the words of the mother that we could hear most clearly were usually the words that the child reproduced. We had trouble hearing the weakly stressed functors and, of course, the child usually failed to reproduce them. Differential stress may then be the cause of the child's differential retention. The outcome is a maximally informative reduction, but the cause of this outcome need not be the making of an information analysis. The outcome may be an incidental consequence of the fact that English is a well-designed language that places its heavier stresses where they are needed, on contentives that cannot easily be guessed from context.

We are fairly sure that differential stress is one of the determinants of the child's telegraphic productions. For one thing, stress will also account for the way in which children reproduce polysyllabic words when the total is too much for them. Adam, for instance, gave us *'pression* for *expression* and Eve gave us *'raff* for *giraffe*; the more heavily-stressed syllables were the ones retained. In addition, we have tried the effect of placing heavy stresses on functors that do not ordinarily receive such stresses. To Adam we said: "You say what I say" and then, speaking in a normal way at first: "The doggie will bite." Adam gave back: "Doggie bite." Then we stressed the auxiliary: "The doggie *will* bite," and after a few trials Adam made attempts at reproducing that auxiliary. A science fiction experiment comes to mind. If there were parents who stressed functors rather than contentives, would they have children whose speech was a kind of "reciprocal telegraphic," made up of articles, prepositions, conjunctions, auxiliaries, and the like? Such children would be out of touch with the community as real children are not.

It may be that all the factors we have mentioned play some part in determining the child's selective imitations: the reference-making function of contentives, the fact that they are practiced as single words, the fact that they cannot be guessed from context, and the heavy stresses they receive. There are also other possible factors; for example, the left-to-right, earlier-to-later position of words in a sentence, but these make too long a story to tell here (Brown and Fraser, 1963). Whatever the causes, the first utterances produced as imitations of adult sentences are highly systematic reductions of their models. Furthermore, the telegraphic properties of these imitations appear also in the child's spontaneously produced utterances. When his speech is not modeled on an immediately prior adult sentence, it observes the same limitation on length and the same predilection for contentives as when it is modeled on an immediately prior sentence.

Imitation with Expansion

In the course of the brief conversation set down in Table 1, Adam's mother at one point imitates Adam. The boy says: "There go one" and mother responds: "Yes, there goes one." She does not exactly reproduce the model sentence of the child but instead adds something to it or expands it. What she adds is a functor, the inflection for third person, to the verb, the very form that Adam had omitted when he imitated his mother.

One of the first things we noticed when we began to study child speech several years ago was the frequency with which adults imitated children. Indeed they seemed to imitate more often than did the children themselves. We later came to realize that adult imitations are seldom exact reproductions; they are usually expansions.

The mothers of Adam and Eve responded to the speech of their children with expansions about 30% of the time. We did it ourselves when we talked with the children. Indeed we found it very difficult to withhold expansions. A reduced or incomplete English sentence seems to constrain the English-speaking adult to expand it into the nearest properly formed complete sentence. Table 3 lists a few sample expansions from the hundreds in the records.

The first thing worthy of attention in the expansions of Table 3 is the fact that the words spoken by the mother

Table 3
EXPANSIONS OF CHILD SPEECH PRODUCED BY MOTHERS

Child	Mother
Baby highchair	*Baby is in the highchair*
Mommy eggnog	*Mommy had her eggnog*
Eve lunch	*Eve is having lunch*
Mommy sandwich	*Mommy'll have a sandwich*
Sat wall	*He sat on the wall*
Throw Daddy	*Throw it to Daddy*
Pick glove	*Pick the glove up*

preserve the order of the words in the child's sentences. To be sure, words and inflections are added, but they are fitted in before, and after, and between the words the child used; they are not generally permitted to disturb the order of the child's words. It is as if these latter were taken as constants by the mother, constants to which some sentence had to be fitted. She acts as if she were assuming that the child means everything he says, all the words and also their order, but as if he might also mean more than he says. From the mother's point of view an expansion is a kind of communication check; it says in effect: "Is this what you mean?"

The second thing to notice about Table 3 is the character of the forms added to the child's utterances. They include the auxiliaries *is* and *will;* the prepositions *in, on, to,* and *up;* the verb forms *is, have, had,* and *having;* the articles *a* and *the;* and the pronouns *her, he,* and *it.* For the most part, the words added are functors, and functors are of course the words that the child omits in his reductions.

The interaction between mother and child, is, much of the time, a cycle of reductions and expansions. There are two transformations involved. The reduction transformation has an almost completely specifiable and so mechanical character. One could program a machine to do it with the following instructions: "Retain contentives (or stressed forms) in the order given up to some limit of length." The expansion accomplished by Adam's mother when she added the third-person inflection to the verb and said, "There goes one," is also a completely specifiable transformation. The instructions would read: "Retain the forms given in the order given and supply obligatory grammatical forms." To be sure this mother-machine would have to be supplied with the obligatory rules of English grammar, but that could be done. However, the sentence "There goes one" is atypical in that it only adds a compulsory and redundant inflection. The expansions of Table 3 all add forms that are not grammatically compulsory or redundant and these expansions cannot be mechanically generated by grammatical rules alone.

In Table 3 the upper four utterances produced by the child are all of the same grammatical type; all four consist of a proper noun followed by a common noun. However, the four are expanded in quite different ways. In particular, the form of the verb changes: it is first in the simple present tense; second in the simple past; third in the present progressive; and last in the simple future. All of these are perfectly grammatical but they are different. The second set of child utterances is formally uniform in that each one consists of a verb followed by a noun. The expansions are again all grammatical but quite unlike, especially with regard to the preposition supplied. In general, then, there are radical changes in the mother's expansions when there are no changes in the formal character of the utterances expanded. It follows that the expansions cannot be produced simply by making grammatically compulsory additions to the child's utterances.

How does a mother decide on the correct expansion of one of her child's utterances? Consider the utterance "Eve lunch." So far as grammar is concerned this utterance could be appropriately expanded in any one of a number of ways: "Eve is having lunch"; "Eve had lunch"; "Eve will have lunch"; "Eve's lunch," and so forth. On the occasion when Eve produced the utterance, however, one expansion seemed more appropriate than any other. It was then the noon hour, Eve was sitting at the table with a plate of food before her and her spoon and fingers were busy. In these circumstances "Eve lunch" had to mean "Eve is having lunch." A little later when the plate had been stacked in the sink and Eve was getting down from her chair the utterance "Eve lunch" would have suggested the expansion "Eve has had her lunch." Most expansions are responsive not only to the child's words but also to the circumstances attending their utterance.

What kind of instructions will generate the mother's expansions? The following are approximately correct: "Retain the words given in the order given, and add those functors that will result in a well-formed simple sentence that is appropriate to the circumstances." These are not instructions that any machine could follow. A machine could act on the instructions only if it were provided with detailed specifications for judging appropriateness, and no such specifications can, at present, be written. They exist, however, in implicit form in the brains of mothers and in the brains of all English-speaking adults, and so judgments of appropriateness can be made by such adults.

The expansion encodes aspects of reality that are not coded by the child's telegraphic utterance. Functors have meaning, but it is meaning that accrues to them in context rather than isolation. The meanings that are added by functors seem to be nothing less than the basic terms in which we construe reality: the time of an action, whether it is ongoing or completed, whether it is presently relevant or not; the concept of possession, and such relational concepts as are coded by *in, on, up, down,* and the like; the difference between a particular instance of a class ("Has anybody seen *the* paper?") and any instance of a class ("Has anybody seen *a* paper?"); the difference between extended substances given shape and size by an "accidental" container (*sand, water, syrup,* etc.) and countable "things" having a characteristic, fixed shape and size (*a cup, a man, a tree,* etc.). It seems to us that a mother, in expanding speech, may be teaching more than grammar; she may be teaching something like a world view.

As yet it has not been demonstrated that expansions are *necessary* for the learning of either grammar or a construction of reality. It has not even been demonstrated that expansions contribute to such learning. All we know is that some parents do expand and their children do learn. It is perfectly possible, however, that children can and do learn simply from hearing their parents or others make well-formed sentences in connection with various nonverbal circumstances. It may not be necessary or even helpful for these sentences to be expansions of utterances of the child. Only experiments contrasting expansion training with simple exposure to English will settle the matter. We hope to do such experiments.

There are, of course, reasons for expecting the expansion transformation to be an effective tutorial technique. By adding something to the words the child has just produced one confirms his response insofar as it is appropriate. In addition one takes him somewhat beyond that response but not greatly beyond it. One encodes additional meanings at a moment when he is most likely to be attending to the cues that can teach that meaning.

Induction of the Latent Structure ✓

Adam, in the course of the conversation with his mother set down in Table 1, produced one utterance for which no adult is likely ever to have provided an exact model: "No I see truck." His mother elects to expand it as "No, you didn't see it" and this expansion suggests that the child might have created the utterance by reducing an adult model containing the form *didn't*. However, the mother's expansion in this case does some violence to Adam's original version. He did not say *no* as his mother said it, with primary stress and final contour; Adam's *no* had secondary stress and no final contour. It is not easy to imagine an adult model for this utterance. It seems more likely that the utterance was created by Adam as part of a continuing effort to discover the general rules for constructing English negatives.

In Table 4 are listed some utterances produced by Adam or Eve for which it is difficult to imagine any

Table 4
UTTERANCES NOT LIKELY TO BE IMITATIONS

My Cromer suitcase	*You naughty are*
Two foot	*Why it can't turn off?*
A bags	*Put on it*
A scissor	*Cowboy did fighting me*
A this truck	*Put a gas in*

adult model. It is unlikely that any adult said any of these to Adam or Eve, since they are very simple utterances and yet definitely ungrammatical. In addition, it is difficult, by adding functors alone, to build any of them up to simple grammatical sentences. Consequently it does not seem likely that these utterances are reductions of adult originals. It is more likely that they are mistakes which externalize the child's search for the regularities of English syntax.

We have long realized that the occurrence of certain kinds of errors on the level of morphology (or word construction) reveals the child's effort to induce regularities from speech. So long as a child speaks correctly, or at any rate so long as he speaks as correctly as the adults he hears, there is no way to tell whether he is simply repeating what he has heard or whether he is actually constructing. However, when he says something like "I digged a hole," we can often be sure that he is constructing. We can be sure, because it is unlikely that he would have heard *digged* from anyone and because we can see how, in processing words he has heard, he might have come by *digged*. It looks like an overgeneralization of the regular past inflection. The inductive operations of the child's mind are externalized in such a creation. Overgeneralizations on the level of syntax (or sentence construction) are more difficult to identify because there are so many ways of adding functors so as to build up conceivable models. But this is difficult to do for the examples of Table 4 and for several hundred other utterances in our records.

The processes of imitation and expansion are not sufficient to account for the degree of linguistic competence that children regularly acquire. These processes alone cannot teach more than the sum total of sentences that speakers of English have either modeled for a child to imitate or built up from a child's reductions.

However, a child's linguistic competence extends far beyond this sum total of sentences. All children are able to understand and construct sentences they have never heard but which are nevertheless well formed, i.e., well formed in terms of general rules that are implicit in the sentences the child has heard. Somehow, then, every child processes the speech to which he is exposed so as to induce from it a latent structure. This latent rule structure is so general that a child can spin out its implications all his life long. It is both semantic and syntactic. The discovery of latent structure is the greatest of the processes involved in language acquisition and the most difficult to understand. We will provide an example of how the analysis can proceed by discussing the evolution in child speech of noun phrases.

A noun phrase in adult English includes a noun, but also more than a noun. One variety consists of a noun with assorted modifiers: *The girl; The pretty girl; That pretty girl; My girl,* and so forth. All of these are constructions that have the same syntactic privileges as do nouns alone. A noun phrase can be used in isolation to name or request something; it can be used in sentences in subject position, or in object position, or in predicate nominative position; all these are slots that a noun alone can also fill. A larger construction having the same syntactic privileges as its "head" word is called, in linguistics, an "endocentric" construction, and noun phrases are endocentric constructions.

For both Adam and Eve, in the early records, noun phrases usually occur as total, independent utterances rather than as components of sentences. Table 5 presents an assortment of such utterances. Each one consists of some sort of modifier, just one, preceding a noun. The modifiers or, as they are sometimes called, the "pivot" words are a much smaller class than the noun class. Three students of child speech (Braine, 1963; Miller and Ervin, 1964; and Brown and Fraser, 1963) have independently discovered that this kind of construction is extremely common when children first begin to combine words.

It is possible to generalize the cases of Table 5 into a simple, implicit rule. The rule symbolized in Table 5

Table 5

NOUN PHRASES IN ISOLATION AND RULE FOR GENERATING NOUN PHRASES AT TIME 1

A coat	*More coffee*
A celery[a]	*More nut*[a]
A Becky[a]	*Two sock*[a]
A hands[a]	*Two shoes*
The top	*Two tinker toy*[a]
My Mommy	*Big boot*
My stool	*Poor man*
That Adam	*Little top*
That knee	*Dirty knee*

$$N P \rightarrow M + N$$

M → *a, big, dirty, little, more, my, poor, that, the, two.*
N → *Adam, Becky, boot, coat, coffee, knee, man, Mommy, nut, sock, stool, tinker toy, top,* and very many others.

[a] Ungrammatical for an adult.

reads: "In order to form a noun phrase of this type, select first one word from the small class of modifiers and select, second, one word from the large class of nouns." This is a "generative" rule, by which we mean that it is a program that would actually serve to build constructions of the type in question. It is offered as a model of the mental mechanism by which Adam and

Eve generated such utterances. Furthermore, judging from our work with other children and from the reports of Braine and of Ervin and Miller, the model describes a mechanism present in many children when their average utterance is approximately two morphemes long.

We have found that even in our earliest records the M + N construction is sometimes used as a component of larger constructions. For instance, Eve said: "Fix a Lassie" and "Turn the page" and "A horsie stuck" and Adam even said: "Adam wear a shirt." There are, at first, only a handful of these larger constructions, but there are very many constructions in which single nouns occur in subject or in object position.

Let us look again at the utterances of Table 5 and the rule generalizing them. The class M does not correspond with any syntactic class of adult English. In the class M are articles, a possessive pronoun, a cardinal number, a demonstrative adjective or pronoun, a quantifier, and some descriptive adjectives—a mixed bag indeed. For adult English these words cannot belong to the same syntactic class because they have very different privileges of occurrence in sentences. For the children the words do seem to function as one class that has the common privilege of occurrence before nouns.

If the initial words of the utterances in Table 5 are treated as one class M, then many utterances are generated which an adult speaker would judge to be ungrammatical. Consider the indefinite article *a*. Adults use it only to modify common count nouns in the singular such as *coat, dog, cup,* and so forth. We would not say *a celery,* or *a cereal,* or *a dirt,* since *celery, cereal,* and *dirt* are mass nouns. We would not say *a Becky* or *a Jimmy,* since *Becky* and *Jimmy* are proper nouns. We would not say *a hands* or *a shoes,* since *hands* and *shoes* are plural nouns. Adam and Eve did, at first, form ungrammatical combinations such as these.

The numeral *two* we use only with count nouns in the plural. We would not say *two sock* since *sock* is singular, nor *two water* since *water* is a mass noun. The word *more* we use before count nouns in the plural (*more nuts*) or before mass nouns in the singular (*more coffee*). Adam and Eve made a number of combinations involving *two* or *more* that we would not make.

Given the initially very undiscriminating use of words in the class M, it follows that one dimension of development must be a progressive differentiation of privileges, which means the division of M into smaller classes. There must also be subdivision of the noun class (N) for the reason that the privileges of occurrence of various kinds of modifiers must be described in terms of such subvarieties of N as the common noun and proper noun, the count noun and mass noun. There must eventually emerge a distinction between nouns singular and nouns plural, since this distinction figures in the privileges of occurrence of the several sorts of modifiers.

Sixteen weeks after our first records from Adam and Eve (Time 2), the differentiation had begun. By this time there were distributional reasons for separating out articles from demonstrative pronouns, and both of these from the residual class of modifiers. Some of the evidence for this conclusion appears in Table 6. In general, one syntactic class is distinguished from another when the members of one class have combinational privileges not enjoyed by the members of the other. Consider, for example, the reasons for distinguishing articles (Art) from modifiers in general (M). Both articles and modifiers appeared in front of nouns in two-word utterances. However, in three-word utterances that were made up from the total pool of words and that had a noun in final position, the privileges of *a* and *the* were different from the privileges of all other modifiers. The articles occurred in initial position followed by a member of class M other than an article. No other modifier occurred in this first position; notice the "Not obtained" examples of Table 6a. If the children had produced utterances

Table 6
SUBDIVISION OF THE MODIFIER CLASS

a. Privileges peculiar to articles	
Obtained	Not Obtained
A blue flower	*Blue a flower*
A nice nap	*Nice a nap*
A your car	*Your a car*
A my pencil	*My a pencil*
b. Privileges peculiar to demonstrative pronouns	
Obtained	Not Obtained
That a horse	*A that horse*
That a blue flower	*A that blue flower*
	Blue a that flower

like those not obtained (for example, *blue a flower*, or *your a car*), there would have been no difference in the privileges of occurrence of articles and modifiers and therefore no reason to separate out articles.

The record of Adam is especially instructive at this

point. He created such notably ungrammatical combinations as "a your car" and "a my pencil." It is very unlikely that adults provided models for these combinations. They argue strongly that Adam regarded all the words in the residual M class as syntactic equivalents and so generated these very odd utterances in which possessive pronouns appear where descriptive adjectives would be more acceptable.

Table 6b also presents some of the evidence for distinguishing demonstrative pronouns (Dem) from articles and modifiers. The pronouns occurred first and ahead of articles in three-and-four-word utterances—a position that neither articles nor modifiers ever filled. The sentences with demonstrative pronouns are recognizable as reductions that omit the copular verb *is*. Such sentences are not noun phrases in adult English, and ultimately they will not function as noun phrases in the speech of the children, but for the present they are not distinguishable distributionally from noun phrases.

Recall now the generative formula of Table 5 which constructs noun phrases by simply placing a modifier (M) before a noun (N). The differentiation of privileges illustrated in Table 6, and the syntactic classes this evidence motivates us to create, complicate the formula for generating noun phrases. In Table 7 we have written a single general formula for producing all noun phrases [NP → (Dem) + (Art) + (M) + N] and also the numerous more specific rules which are summarized by the general formula.

By the time of the 13th transcription, 26 weeks after we began our study, privileges of occurrence were much more finely differentiated, and consequently syntactic classes were more numerous. From the distributional evidence we judged that Adam had made five classes of his original class M: articles, descriptive adjectives,

Table 7

RULES FOR GENERATING NOUN PHRASES AT TIME 2

$NP_1 \rightarrow Dem + Art + M + N$
$NP_2 \rightarrow Art + M + N$
$NP_3 \rightarrow Dem + M + N$
$NP_4 \rightarrow Art + N$
$NP_5 \rightarrow M + N$
$NP_6 \rightarrow Dem + N$ $\qquad$ $NP \rightarrow (Dem)^a + (Art) + (M) + N$

[a] Class within parentheses is optional.

possessive pronouns, demonstrative pronouns, and a residual class of modifiers. The generative rules of Table 7 had become inadequate; there were no longer, for instance, any combinations like "a your car." Eve had the same set, except that she used two residual classes of modifiers. In addition, nouns had begun to subdivide for both children. The usage of proper nouns had become clearly distinct from the usage of count nouns. For Eve the evidence justified separating count nouns from mass nouns, but for Adam it still did not. Both children by this time were frequently pluralizing nouns, but as yet their syntactic control of the singular-plural distinction was imperfect.

In summary, one major aspect of the development of general structure in child speech is a progressive differentiation in the usage of words and therefore a progressive differentiation of syntactic classes. At the same time, however, there is an integrative process at work.

From the first, an occasional noun phrase occurred as a component of some larger construction. At first these noun phrases were just two words long, and the range of positions in which they could occur was small. With time the noun phrases grew longer, were more frequently used, and were used in a greater range of positions. The noun-phrase structure as a whole, in all the permissible combinations of modifiers and nouns, was assuming the combinational privileges enjoyed by nouns in isolation.

In Table 8 are set down some of the sentence positions in which both nouns and noun phrases occurred

Table 8
SOME PRIVILEGES OF THE NOUN PHRASE

Noun Positions	Noun-Phrase Positions
That (flower)	*That (a blue flower)*
Where (ball) go?	*Where (the puzzle) go?*
Adam write (penguin)	*Doggie eat (the breakfast)*
(Horsie) stop	*(A horsie) crying*
Put (hat) on	*Put (the red hat) on*

in the speech of Adam and Eve. It is the close match between the positions of nouns alone and of nouns with modifiers in the speech of Adam and Eve that justifies us in calling the longer constructions noun phrases. These longer constructions are, as they should be, endocentric; the head word alone has the same syntactic privileges as the head word with its modifiers. The continuing absence, in noun-phrase positions, of whole constructions of the type, "That a blue flower," signals the fact that these constructions are telegraphic versions of predicate nominative sentences, with the verb form *is* omitted. Examples of the kind of construction not obtained are: "That (that a blue flower)," or "Where (that a blue flower)?"

For adults the noun phrase is a subwhole of the sentence, what linguists call an "immediate constituent." The noun phrase has a kind of psychological unity. There are signs that the noun phrase was also an immediate constituent for Adam and Eve. Consider the sentence with the separable verb *put on*. The noun phrase in "Put the red hat on" is, as a whole, fitted in between the verb and the particle, even as is the noun alone in "Put hat on." What is more, however, the location of pauses in the longer sentence on several occasions suggested the psychological organization, "Put . . . the red hat . . . on," rather than "Put the red . . . hat on," or "Put the . . . red hat on." In addition to this evidence, the use of pronouns suggests that the noun phrase is a psychological unit.

The unity of noun phrases in adult English is evidenced, in the first place, by the syntactic equivalence between such phrases and nouns alone. It is evidenced, in the second place, by the fact that pronouns are able to substitute for total noun phrases. In our immediately preceding sentence the pronoun "It" stands for the rather involved construction: "The unity of noun phrases in adult English." The words called "pronouns" in English would more aptly be called "pro-noun-phrases" since it is the phrase rather than the noun that they usually replace. One does not replace "unity" with "it" and say "The *it* of noun phrases in adult English." In the speech of Adam and Eve, too, the pronoun came to function as a replacement for the noun phrase. Some of the clearer cases appear in Table 9.

Table 9

PRONOUNS REPLACING NOUNS OR NOUN PHRASES, AND PRONOUNS PRODUCED TOGETHER WITH NOUNS OR NOUN PHRASES

Noun Phrases Replaced by Pronouns	Pronouns and Noun Phrases in Same Utterances
Hit ball	Mommy get it ladder
Get it	Mommy get it my ladder
Ball go?	Saw it ball
Go get it	Miss it garage
Made it	I miss it cowboy boot
Made a ship	I Adam drive that
Fix a tricycle	I Adam drive
Fix it	I Adam don't

Adam characteristically externalizes more of his learning than does Eve and his record is especially instructive in connection with the learning of pronouns. In his first eight records, taken during the first 16 weeks of the study, Adam quite often produced sentences containing both the pronoun and the noun or noun phrase that the pronoun should have replaced. One can see here the equivalence in process of establishment. First the substitute is produced and then, as if in explication, the form or forms that will eventually be replaced by the substitute. Adam spoke out his pronoun antecedents as chronological consequents. This is additional evidence of the unity of the noun phrase, since the noun phrases *my ladder* and *cowboy boot* are linked with *it* in Adam's speech in just the same way as the nouns *ladder* and *ball*.

We have described three processes involved in the

child's acquisition of syntax. It is clear that the last of these, the induction of latent structure, is by far the most complex. It looks as if this last process will put a serious strain on any learning theory thus far conceived by psychology. The very intricate simultaneous differentiation and integration that constitutes the evolution of the noun phrase is more reminiscent of the biological development of an embryo than it is of the acquisition of a conditioned reflex.

REFERENCES

Braine, M. D. S. The ontogeny of English phrase structure: The first phase. *Language,* 1963, **39,** 1-13.

Brown, R., and Fraser, C. The acquisition of syntax. In C. N. Cofer and Barbara S. Musgrave (Editors), *Verbal behavior and learning.* New York: McGraw-Hill, 1963.

Maclay, H., and Osgood, C. E. Hesitation phenomena in spontaneous English speech. *Word,* 1959, **15,** 19-44.

Miller, W., and Ervin, S. The development of grammar in child language. In U. Bellugi and R. Brown (Editors), The acquisition of language. *Child Developm. Monogr.,* 1964, **29,** 9-34.

SUSAN M. ERVIN*

Imitation and Structural Change in Children's Language

We all know that children's grammar converges on
the norm for the community in which they live. How
does this happen? One source might be through adult
correction of errors and through operant conditioning
reinforced by the responses of others. This is probably
a relatively weak source of change in first language
learning. We know, for instance, that children learn
certain grammatical structures which nobody taught
them explicitly, and we also know that often teachers
try hard to eradicate some of them. All over the world
children learn grammatical patterns whether or not
anyone corrects their speech, and there have been cases
in which children who were believed for years to be
mute have been found employing relatively mature
grammatical patterns. A second source of change is
maturation. Young children cannot learn grammatical

* University of California at Berkeley.

and semantic concepts of a certain degree of complexity, and they produce sentences limited in length. Gvozdev (1961), in a book on child language development in Russian, has presented evidence that, when grammatical complexity is held constant, semantic difficulty is related to the age of acquisition of certain grammatical patterns. For instance, the conditional is learned late. Recent work by Roger W. Brown and his group supports this view. But maturation cannot account for the content of language nor for the particular structures acquired. A third factor affecting language development might be comprehension. We know that, typically, recognition precedes production. We know that people can understand many more words than they ever use. The number of cues for recognition is less than the information needed for accurate production, and in recognition we can often profit from redundancy.

Fraser, Bellugi, and Brown (1963) have recently found that children's imitation of grammatical contrasts regularly surpassed their comprehension, which in turn was superior to their freely generated speech. For instance, they would choose the right picture, or repeat "The sheep are jumping," or "The sheep is jumping," more often than they could speak the right name when a picture was pointed out.

The children in this study were asked to imitate. The real test as to whether imitation is significant as a source of progress in grammar should be based on spontaneous imitations, for children may imitate selectively.

The material to be reported here is merely suggestive.

It consists of a study of only five children.* It is unique in that I have the advantage of working from careful descriptive grammars for each of the children about whom I shall report. The crucial test is this: Are imitated utterances grammatically different from free utterances? If they are different, are they more advanced grammatically?

Ideally, one would write independent grammars for the imitated sentences and for the freely generated sentences and compare the grammatical rules. Since the number of imitations was far too small, grammatical rules were written only for the free sentences, and then the imitations were tested for their consistency with these rules. This method loads the dice against the similarity of the imitations to the free sentences.

First I shall describe what I mean by a grammar, then define what I mean by imitation, and finally test the hypothesis of similarity.

We collected 250 sentences of two words or more from Donnie (Table 1). At this time, when he was 2 years and 2 months old, his mother reported that he had just begun to put words together. The rule described here accounts for 198 of Donnie's sentences.

Another 16 sentences followed another rule, producing "what's that" and "what's this." There were 35 sentences which could be described by neither rule.

* Conducted with the support of a grant from the National Institute of Mental Health and the facilities of the Institute for Human Development and the Institute for Human Learning at the University of California, Berkeley. The work was done in collaboration with Wick Miller, now Assistant Professor of Anthropology at the University of Utah.

Table 1

SENTENCE-GENERATING RULE FOR DONNIE, AGE 2:2

Optional Classes[a]						Required Class
1	2	3	4	5	6	7
goodness					bead	bead(s)
oh	here(s)				blanket	blanket
oh oh	there(s)	go[b]			bow-wow	bow-wow
oh dear	where(s)		a		car	car(s)
				big	choochoo	choochoo
see			the		Daddy	Daddy
whee	this				kiddy-car	kiddy-car
	that(s)				ring	ring
					truck	truck(s)
					water	water
					etc.	etc.

  [a] Classes 1 to 6, selected in that order, may precede 7.
  [b] "This" and "that(s)" never precede "go."

You will see that the following sentences were grammatically consistent:

Blanket water.	Oh, there's a bed.
Bow-wow dog.	Oh, car.
Here big truck.	Oh, dear, the truck.
Where go the car?	Where's a big choochoo car?

We could not account for 7 per cent of Donnie's sentences by any simple rules. These included the following:

Where the more bead?	Go bye-bye Daddy.
Naughty Donnie.	Here's it go.
Go get the truck.	Here's it goes.
What the choochoo car?	

Three months later, Donnie's grammar had changed (Table 2). Some of the sentences that we could not account for at the earlier stage have now become more frequent and stable. We now find it necessary to set up a phrase rule for a nominal phrase, which you see in

Table 2. Although all the regular sentences at the younger age contained at least one nominal, there are now more frequent sentences without a nominal phrase

Table 2
NOMINAL PHRASE-GENERATING RULE FOR DONNIE, AGE 2:5

	Optional Classes[a]			Required Class
	1	2	3	4
NOMINAL	a the	red big more	all-gone ball bead broken bye-bye choochoo green monkey truck yellow etc.	all-gone ball bead(s) broken bye-bye choochoo green monkey truck yellow etc.

[a] Classes 1 to 3, in that order, may precede 4.

(Table 3). We can conveniently divide Donnie's sentences into four types at this age. The largest number, 173, were declarative sentences like "there's a bus," "there's a green," "here's a broken," and "there's all-gone." Ninety-six were nominal sentences like "big

Table 3
SENTENCE-GENERATING RULE FOR DONNIE, AGE 2:5

1	2	3[a]	4	5	6
oh boy hi no don't etc.	there(s) where(s) here(s) that(s) [b] this is[b]	it all NOMINAL	go goes	NOMINAL	have-it[c]

[a] Multiword sentences contain at least one item from columns 3 to 6, with order as in the sequence of columns.
[b] That(s) and this (is) never precede columns 4 to 6.
[c] Columns 4 and 6 are mutually exclusive.

yellow," "oh, broken," "yellow broken," or "monkey broken." Another 76 contained "go" or "goes" as in "car go broken," "goes the bubbles," and "there's it go." There were 20 sentences with "have-it," meaning "I want it." For example, "there beads, have-it" and "where the choo-choo, have-it."

These are inductive or descriptive rules or grammars. Alternative descriptions might do as well: our criteria were brevity and completeness. We can test a grammar of an adult language by asking speakers if test sentences are acceptable; with so-called dead, literary languages we can cross-check different sources. With children, our descriptions must be more tentative. For these two-year-olds we found that between 77 and 80 per cent of the sentences could be described by our grammars.

Now we turn to the central issue. Are the spontaneous imitations of these children governed by the same rules as their freely generated sentences? To illustrate, here are some examples of Donnie's imitations at 2.5. You will find the first three are consistent, the last two are not. The first column is the model, the second the imitation.

"This is a round ring."	"This ring."
"Where does it go?"	"Where's it go?"
"Is Donnie all-gone?"	"Donnie all-gone."
"Is it a bus?"	"It a bus."
"Is it broken?"	"Is broken?"

We have confined this study only to overt, immediate repetitions. We have excluded imitations in which there were changes, as in "Liz is naughty," "He's naughty." We found that adult conversations are heavily threaded with such partial imitations and also that they are hard to separate from answers to questions. Judges might easily disagree in judging which were imitations. We kept the clear-cut cases, including exact repetitions, which were few, echoes of the final few words in sentences, repetitions with words omitted, and the few instances of repetitions with changes in word order. Omissions bulked large in our cases of imitation. These tended to be concentrated on the unstressed segments of sentences, on articles, prepositions, auxiliaries, pronouns, and suffixes. For instance: "I'll make a cup for her to drink" produced "cup drink"; "Mr. Miller will try," "Miller try"; "Put the strap under her chin," "Strap chin." Thus the imitations had three characteristics: they selected the most recent and most emphasized words, and they preserved the word order.

When the imitations have been isolated, the next step is to identify the grammatically consistent sentences. These were of two types. Some used vocabulary that we had included in describing the grammars. As I have said, our rules included lists of words according to classes, or by positions they could occupy. Some of the imitated sentences included new words that were not on these lists. Any speech sample is selective in vocabulary, and since we were interested in structure and not vocabulary, we arbitrarily included as grammatical any sentences containing a single new word by treating these words as "deuces wild." That is to say, any new word could be assigned to a class so as to make a grammatical sentence. The same rule was used on the residual sentences which were freely generated. Some of these sentences were called ungrammatical simply because they included grammatically ambiguous words.

We used exactly the same rule of procedure for the imitated sentences and for the free sentences in deciding whether the sentence fit the structural rules or not. We made liberal, but equally liberal, provision for accepting new vocabulary in both samples. Thus we can see whether the rules of word arrangement were the same in the two samples (Table 4).

For all the children except one, Holly, the sentences in both samples were equally predictable from both rules. Donnie was studied at three ages, and there was no change with age in the consistency of his imitated sentences.

But what about Holly? We must move to our second question with her: Were the imitated sentences grammatically more advanced than the free ones, or simply more inconsistent? We shall use three criteria in judging

Table 4
GRAMMATICAL NOVELTY OF IMITATIONS

	Percentage Imitated	Percentage Grammatically Consistent	
		Freely Generated	Imitated
Susan (1.10)	7	88	79
Christy (2.0)	5	91	92
Donnie (2.2)	6	93	100
Lisa (2.3)	15	83	65
Holly (2.4)	20	88	68[a]
Donnie (2.5)	8	91	94
Donnie (2.10)	7	92	91

[a] $X^2 = 9.4$

the grammatical maturity of these sentences. These criteria are based on the changes that characterized the children's speech in the months following those we are considering. First, sentence length increased with age. Donnie's sentences at the three ages considered had an average length of 2.2, 2.4, and 2.7 words. Secondly, there is an increase in certain grammatical markers with age, including an increase in the use of articles and pronouns. Finally, there is an increase in adult-like sentence constructions consisting of imperative-plus-object, or subject-verb-object, or subject-verb-adjective, or subject-verb-particle. Examples are "hold it," "he took it," "that's hot," and "they came over."

Using these three criteria, we examined all of Holly's residual sentences, both imitated and free, that did *not* fit the rules of arrangement we had called her grammar. The average length of the free sentences was three words, of the imitated sentences, two words. There were grammatical markers such as articles and pronouns in 62 per cent of the free sentences, and in 28 per cent of the imitated sentences. Half of the free sentences and a third of the imitated sentences were structurally complete, from an adult standpoint. There were no subject-verb-object imitated sentences, but there were six subject-verb-object free sentences, such as "I want play game" and "I don't see Heather car," Heather being Holly's sister.

We are left with a question about why Holly was so different from the other children. It was something of a *tour de force* to write a grammar for Holly. One class, identified as a class by the fact that its members occupied initial position in sentences, included "this-one," "see," "want" and "there." Another heterogeneous class, identified only by the fact that it followed the words just described, include "around," "pull," "raining," "book," and "two." No other child had such a bizarre system, if system it was. Probably Holly's imitations did not fit this system because these were not in fact rules governing her speech. Donnie's rules were far more simple, consistent, and pervasive. It is possible that the high percentage of imitations produced by Holly is related to the fluidity of her grammar. But if it is so, then her imitations were a disturbing rather than a productive factor in her grammatical development.

If we can rely at all on this sample of five children, there is an inescapable conclusion. Imitations under the optimal conditions, those of immediate recall, are not grammatically progressive. We cannot look to overt imitation as a source for the rapid progress children make in grammatical skill in these early years.

A word of caution. I have *not* said that imitation is never important in language learning. In comprehension covert imitation may be important. Possibly imitation aids in the acquisition of vocabulary or of phonetic mastery. Perhaps overt imitation is indispensable in the special conditions of classroom language learning. All I have said is that there is not a shred of evidence supporting a view that progress toward adult norms of grammar arises merely from practice in overt imitation of adult sentences.

Fitting Theories to Facts

One may take several different approaches in accounting for child language development. We have already touched on one: the imitative view. According to this conceptualization the child makes errors and introduces abbreviations in his effort to approximate sentences he hears. Development is thought to consist of gradual elimination of such random errors.

This point of view is implied in the studies of grammatical development which have counted grammatical errors, omissions, and sentence length as criteria for developmental level. A second view assumes that children have sets of rules like those of adults, since they can understand adults, but that in speaking they have a combination of editing rules and random production errors. Development consists in eliminating the omissions and redundancies arising from these editing rules. A third view would assume that development can be described as the evolution of a series of linguistic systems increasing in complexity, with changes in behavior reflecting changes in the child's syntactical rules.

The data reported below have been collected in a collaborative study with Wick Miller, in which frequent texts were collected from seven monolingual oldest children, and monthly systematic tests were conducted on 24 children, during a period approximately from age 2 to 4.

In English plural inflection, the contrast *dogs* vs. *dog* might be learned as if the two words were unrelated, separate items of vocabulary. Each would be learned by imitation and by association with the appropriate semantic discrimination. Yet imitation will not account for the behavior of adults speaking English. If an adult hears a new word, say, the name of a new tool, such as a *mindon*, he will surely call two of them *mindons*, a word he has never heard. We might say that he has formed a new word by analogy. Such analogic extensions are not explainable as simple generalization, because they occur when both the referent and the word itself are new and clearly distinguishable from previously known words. We found that children formed new plurals in this way when they were between 2 and 3 years old.

We tested children systematically by showing them objects, first singly and then in pairs, and asking for a description. These tests were conducted at monthly intervals. Some of the things we asked about were familiar, such as "boys" and "oranges." Others were new objects, called such things as a *bik*, *pud*, or *bunge*.

If the child learns the plural first in terms of separate items of vocabulary, we would expect him to employ the plural suffix with some consistency with familiar words before he generalized to new words. In fact, this is just what happened. For nearly all the children, there was a time gap between the time when a familiar plural was used and the time when an analogous new word was given a plural. Thus, between the time when the child contrasted *block* and *blocks* and the time when he said that two things called *bik* were *biks*, there was a small but reliable gap of about two weeks. For *car* and *boy* and the analogous *kie,* the gap was about six weeks. For other words the gap was greater. In all cases—*pud, bik, kie, tass,* and *bunge*—the new contrast appeared later than the contrasts the children had heard.

We would expect that this extension to new forms also would occur for the irregular plurals. All of the children, over the period we studied them, regularized the plural for *foot* and *man.* They said *man-mans,* and *foot-foots* or *feet-feets.* Most preferred *foot-foots.* Very few of the children fluctuated between *foot* and *feet,* so although the word *feet* must have been heard by the children, we can clearly see a regularizing influence. If imitation alone were at work, we would have expected fluctuation between *foot* and *feet.*

There was a difference in the time of acquisition depending on form. The English plural form is quite regular and has few exceptions. Its form is governed by certain sound rules. Thus we have *mat* and *mats,* but *match* and *matches.* We can describe this difference by saying that words ending in sibilants, such as *horse, buzz, match, judge, marsh,* or *rouge,* add a vowel plus *s.* Children at this age frequently do not distinguish these sounds phonetically—orange may be pronounced unpredictably as *orinch, orinz, orints, orins, orinsh* by the same child. The children all shared the problem of adding *s* to words ending in sibilant sounds. What they did was omit a plural contrast for these words. The usual pattern in the earlier grammars was distinction of singular and plural except for words ending in sibilants, which had the same forms for singular and plural.

Occasionally we would have analogies which removed
the sibilant, as in singular *bun* plural *buns* for *bunges*,
and singular *bok* plural *boks* for *boxes*.

At some point each child produced the regular plural
for one of these sibilant words. Quite often, when this
happened, the plural for other earlier forms changed.
Thus when *box-boxes* first was given, we found such
forms as *foot-footses*, or *hand-handses*. Another pattern
sometimes appeared. When *tass-tasses* came in, we found
foot-footiz or *bik-bikiz*.

These changes occurred with children who had previously used the *-s* plural regularly, for *foot*, *bik*, and
hand. Why did these words change? If we examine
the whole range of plurals employed at one of these
points in time, we might describe the system as involving two plural forms vacillating unpredictably from *-s*
to *-iz*. Alternatively, *-s* or *siz* were both in unpredictable
variation. Surely, at this point, it is clear that the child
is employing some common response, whatever you may
call it, in using all of these plural forms. A linguist
would say the child had a plural morpheme with two
allomorphs in free variation. How can a psychologist
translate this behavior into terms familiar to him? This
is most certainly not behavior learned by accumulated
imitation. It is transitory, lasting at most two months,
and then is resolved into a system of conditioned variation like that of adults.

There are two pieces of evidence here which will not
fit a theory that inflection develops through imitation of
familiar forms and extension by generalization to new
items. One is the fact that *foot* and *feet* do not fluctuate

as much as imitation of adults would lead us to expect. The other is that even highly practiced, familiar plurals may be temporarily changed in form by overgeneralization of new patterns. Both these data suggest that analogy in the production of sentences is a very important process and may outweigh the imitation of familiar forms.

Analogy is a familiar process to linguists. Formal similarity is the basis for the construct they call a morpheme. Yet overlaid on the child's systematic analogic forms, or morphemic patterns, we have a gradual accumulation of successful imitations which do not fit the stabilized pattern of the child, in such instances as *oranges* and *boxes*. Eventually these result in a change in the system, which becomes evident in the errors, from the adult standpoint, and in the analogic extensions to nonsense words. The conditioned allomorphs in the adult system—the different plurals in *mats* and *matches* —were imitated one by one at first. Then they produced random fluctuation between the two forms, and later stable responses conditioned by the same features in the phonetic environment as the adult plurals.

Now let us turn to past tense inflection. Our best data are from the group of seven children from whom we collected extensive texts in interviews over a period of time. It is, of course, much harder to elicit a contrast in tense than one in plurality. The semantic cues are less controllable. For this reason we relied on less systematic methods of testing. Now it happens that the English tense system has analogies to the system of plurals. Like the plurals, it has both a regular pattern and irregular forms. There is *walk-walked*, and there is *go-went*. As with the plurals, the specific phonemic pattern depends on the particular final phoneme of the simple verb—we have *pack-packed* and *pat-patted*, when a vowel is added in the suffix. As with plurals, the children used forms that indicated the difficulty of the pattern of adding a vowel—forms such as *toasteded*.

The major formal difference in English between plural inflection of nouns and tense inflection of verbs is the great frequency of irregular (or strong) verbs, whereas irregular nouns are relatively few. It was a surprise to me, in examining verb frequency tables for the children we studied, to find that verbs with regular inflection were few and infrequent in our earliest texts. Therefore, tense inflection begins with the *irregular* forms.

I looked for the first case of extension of the regular past tense suffix which could not have been imitated—for instance *buyed, comed, doed*. The odd, and to me astonishing thing is that these extensions occurred in some cases before the child had produced *any* other regular past tense forms according to our sample. In some cases the other past tense forms consisted of only one or two words of dubious significance as past tense signals.

Relatively rare was the extension of irregular patterns—though we did find *tooken*. With plurals we had found that extension to new instances followed considerable practice with the regular pattern. Of course, our texts must underestimate the frequency of regular verbs, since they are small samples, but the regularity with which we found such extensions occurring quite early suggests that it takes relatively few instances and little practice to produce analogic extension. Another interpretation is that such extensions can occur with little or no actual contrasts in the child's speech; he may base them on the variety of types employing the regular contrast in the language of the adult. That is, if he can comprehend the contrast in the adult language he may on that basis be led to produce analogous forms.

With plurals, the regular patterns were learned and extended first; children did not waver between *foot-feet* and *foot-foots* but employed *foot-foots* normally. With the irregular past tense forms, the children learned the unique, irregular contrasts as separate items of vocabulary first. Sometimes they were separate even contextually, as in the child who said *it came off* and *it came unfastened,* but *come over here* and *come right back.* Next, the children produced analogic past tense forms for these highly frequent words. At the same period in which a child said *did,* he might say *doed*; at the same age at which he said *broke,* he might say *breaked,* and so on. We do not know if there were correlated linguistic or semantic differences between these two versions of the past tense forms. At any event, these productive analogies occurred before we had evidence of practice on the familiar forms from which the analogies presumably stemmed. Whatever its basis in practice, it seems clear that the regularizing or analogizing tendency is very strong.

The learning of syntax is even more difficult to explain. Let us go back before the age of two. In the earliest examples we have obtained, we find that there are consistencies of order between words. A very simple system might be one that produces sentences like *all-gone candy, candy up-there, all-gone book, read book*, and *book read*. Another said *snap on, snap off, fix on*. Notice that these sentences could not all be produced by simple abbreviation of adult sentences. Many of the children's sentences are such imitations, but some have a word order that cannot be explained by simple imitation. Children talk a great deal and they hear a great deal. It is improbable that they could produce the great variety of sentences they do produce from memorized strings of words.

When we introduced words to a child in controlled sentences, he put them into new and appropriate sentences. When told of a nonsense object *that's a po*, or *this is a po*, the child said *here's a po, where's a po, there's a po, the po go up there*, and *poz go up there*. When told *I'm gonna sib the toy*, he later said *I sib 'em*, indicating the appropriate gesture. Yet the form *wem*, in *this is a wem bead*, was not extended. Thus a noun form was productively utilized in many new contexts, a verb form in one, and an adjective form in none. However slight, at least here is an indication of an analogic extension at the syntactic level.

One explanation which has been offered by several different observers of young children, for instance, Braine (1963), Brown and Fraser (1963), and Miller and Ervin (1964), is that these early systems indicate the beginnings of syntactic classes.

How do such classes develop? Two features of classes have been noted to account for the development of regularities. In children's language, there is greater semantic consistency than in adult language. Brown (1957) has shown that by nursery school age children identify verbs with action, nouns with things. Perhaps groupings into classes of words that can occur in the same place in sentences rest at least partly on semantic similarities. Another feature is that in all these grammars there are some positions where only a few words can occur, but that these words are very frequent. Thus one child started many of her sentences with *thats*. Another ended many of her sentences with *on* or *off*. The words that can occur following *thats* constitute a class, in the same sense that nouns are identified as following *the* for adults. This is not the only way we recognize nouns, but it is almost as useful as a suffix in marking the class. How do we know that these words "go together" in a class for the child? We find that the recorded bed-time monologues of a child described by Weir (1962) were filled with instances of words substituting for each other: *what color blanket, what color mop, what color glass; there is the light; here is the light; where is the light.* Such practice, like the second-language drill in the classroom, could make some words equivalent counters in the game of rearrangement we call language. Thus, both meaning and high frequency of certain linguistic environments seem important in the evolution of syntactic classes.

Clearly, we have evidence that children are creative at the very beginnings of sentence formation. They imitate a great deal, but they also produce sentences which have both regularity and systematic difference from adult patterns. At the same time, within these classes there are always statistical tendencies toward finer differentiations.

As my last example, I will take the grammatical features called transformations by Chomsky (1957). A good instance is the rule for the purely syntactical use of *do* in English. This word appears in a variety of sentence types: in elliptical forms, such as *yes, they do,* in emphatic forms such as *they do like it,* in questions such as *do they like it?* and in negatives as in *they don't like it.* According to Chomsky's analysis, these uses of *do* are analogous and can be described by a single set of related rules in the grammar of adult English.

Let us see how children employ *do.* In the negative, a simple rule for the contrast of affirmative and negative would be simply to add *no* or *not* in a specified place. *He's going* vs. *he's not going*; *he has shoes* vs. *he has no shoes.* Another procedure would be to contrast *is* with *isn't, can* with *can't,* and so on. In both cases, the contrast of affirmative and negative rests on a simple addition or change, analogous to the morphological change for tense or for the plural. Neither rule presents new problems.

Some children had several co-existing negative signals. During the time period, one child had the following: (1) *any* in possession sentences, such as *Joe has any sock* and *all the children has any shirt on*; (2) *not* in descriptions and declaratives, such as *not Polly*; (3) *don't* in most verb sentences, such as *don't eat that,* and *I don't like that.* Note that all these utterances can be described in very simple terms without the use of more complex constructs than those needed to account for inflection, or simple syntactic classes.

But as the child acquires verb inflection, more complex rules develop. We say *he goes,* but we do not usually say *he goes not.* Simple addition of *not* is inadequate. We say *he doesn't go.* In the contrast *he can go* vs. *he can't go* there is only one difference. In the contrast *he goes* vs. *he doesn't go* there are two: the addition of the word *don't* in appropriate number and tense, and the difference between *go* and *goes.*

Usually children use *don't* quite early as a negative signal, but as inflections began we found sentences like *Joe doesn't likes it* and *it doesn't fits in there.* In these sentences inflections appeared, but in two places. In an analogous development, *do* appeared early in elliptical sentences as a verb substitute. Thus we find, in response to the remark *there aren't any blocks in this book,* the reply *there do,* and when Wick Miller said *I'm Joe,* the child said *no you don't, you're Wick.* Thus the child had not differentiated subclasses of words used in elliptical constructions, just as the subclasses of inflections of *do* with different number and tense did not appear until later. By age three, this child said *it goes right here, doesn't it?* and *you're named "she," aren't you?,* employing complex constructions which cannot be explained in terms of the simple semantic signals we found in *Joe has any sock.*

Chomsky has described the various uses of *do* in adult English economically as based on the same rule. Does the use of *do* appear concurrently in negatives, interrogatives, ellipsis, and emphasis? Quite clearly this is not the case. As we have seen, *don't* appears early in negatives. It is often the only negative signal. In interrogatives, the question is signaled by question words or by a rising pitch, and *do* is typically not present until months after it appears in negatives or in ellipsis. Thus we cannot infer the process of acquisition from an analysis of the structure of the adult language. Sentences that are described as generated through transformation rules in the adult grammar may be based on different, and simpler, rules in the early stages of the child's grammar. And a rule that may apply to a variety of types of sentences in the adult grammar may develop through quite separate and independent rules in the early stages of the children's grammars.

I have mentioned the development of tense and number inflection, simple syntax, and more complex syntactical processes called transformations. These have all raised certain similar problems of explanation.

In adult language, it has been found necessary to postulate such constructs as morpheme classes, syntactic classes, and grammatical rules. It is not inevitable that similar constructs need be employed in accounting for the earliest stages of language acquisition.

Three different theories of child language development were described earlier. The imitation view assumed that the child imitates adult sentences and gradually eliminates abbreviations and errors as he grows older. A second view assume that children comprehend adult rules but make random errors in speaking. A third view sees language in children as involving successive systems, with increasing complexity.

In their simplest forms all these positions seem wrong. Let us review the evidence. We found that spontaneous imitations were syntactically similar to or simpler than nonimitations. In examining plural inflection, we saw that indiscriminate imitation would lead us to predict free variation of *foot* and *feet*, but, in fact, one form was usually preferred, and the plural contrast was based on analogic extension. We found it necessary to postulate a plural morpheme to account for the sudden and transitory appearance of forms like *bockis* and *feetsiz*. With verbs, mere frequency of use of a contrast was less important than the variety of types employing it, suggesting again the need for conditions giving rise to a past-tense morpheme, with varied environments for a particular form, before analogic extension can occur.

In children's early syntax, the data are still ambiguous, for it is hard to elicit and identify extensions to new cases. On the one hand, sentences like *fix on, allgone puzzle, I not got red hair,* and *once I made a nothing pie* clearly involve processes of analogic extension. Here we see at least rudimentary classes. On the other hand, in any system we devised, there were indications of incipient subdivision, of statistical irregularities in the direction of the adult model, prior to shifts in the system.

In the use of *do* we found that the adult rule applies equally to the negative, interrogative, elliptical, and emphatic sentence. But among children *do* did not appear at the same time in these types of sentences. The pattern of development, and the rules that might describe usage at a particular point in time, differed for these different sentence types and differed for different children. Yet there were rules; errors were not random.

In all these cases, we find that children seem to be disposed to create linguistic systems. We have not examined the speech of twins, but it seems likely that we would find there a rich source of systematic creation of constructions. It is hard to conceive that children could, by the age of four, produce the extraordinarily complex and original sentences we hear from them if they were not actively, by analogic extensions, forming classes and rules.

At the same time we cannot wholly accept the third position presented—that of idiosyncratic systems. In every instance of systematic change I have examined, there has been some evidence of fluctuation, some evidence of greater similarity to adult speech than one would expect on the basis of the system alone. In addition, in the early stages of some complex rules—such as the use of *do*—we found that there were phases that seemed to rest on rudimentary acquisition of vocabulary. The use of *don't* as an undifferentiated negative signal could be so described.

The shift from one system to another may be initiated from several sources. One is the comprehension of adult speech, another is imitation. The relation of imitation to comprehension has barely been faced in discussions of child language, yet these two must account for the accretion of instances which eventuate in systematic changes.

In language, unlike other intellectual processes, the child can monitor his output through the same channel by which he receives the speech of others. If he knows how—if he can make discriminations and remember models—he can compare his own speech to that of others. Thus, language development involves at least three processes.

It is obvious that there is continual expansion in the comprehension of adult speech. Perhaps comprehension requires some ability to anticipate and hence, at a covert level, involves some of the same behavior that occurs in speech production. But this practice in comprehension alone is not sufficient to bring overt speech into conformity with understood speech. Consider again the phenomenon of so-called twin languages, for instance, or the language skills of second-generation immigrants who have never spoken the parents' first language but understand it, or of second-language learners who persistently make certain errors of syntax after years of second-language dominance, or of some children of immigrants who understand their age peers but speak the English of their parents. More than comprehension is involved.

Another process is the imitation of particular instances by children. What is entailed in hearing and imitation we do not know at this point. The fact that phrases may be uttered long after they are heard, without overt practice, suggests that our study of immediate, spontaneous imitation concerns only a fraction of actual imitation-derived utterances. Yet unless these utterances constitute a systematically simpler sample of all imitated utterances, it is obvious from our analysis of them that syntactical development at least cannot rest on imitation.

The third process is the building by analogy of classes and rules, a process which we infer from the child's consistent production of sentences he could not have heard. Of the three approaches which I offered earlier, I would suggest that the third is closest to the truth, but that the accrual of gradual changes under the influence of listening to adults lies at the base of the generalizations and analogies formed by the child. Any system of analysis which omits either the idiosyncratically structured and rule-governed features of children's language or the gradual changes within these rules is contradicted by evidence from all levels of the linguistic behavior of children.

REFERENCES

Braine, Martin D. S., The ontogeny of English phrase structure: The first phase. *Language,* 1963, **39**, 1-13.

Brown, R. Linguistic determination and the part of speech. *J. abnorm. soc. Psychol.,* 1957, **55**, 1-5.

Brown, R., and Fraser, C., The acquisition of syntax. In C. N. Cofer and Barbara Musgrave (Editors), *Verbal behavior and learning.* New York: McGraw-Hill, 1963.

Chomsky, N. *Syntactic structures.* The Hague: Mouton, 1957.

Fraser, C., Bellugi, U., and Brown, R. Control of grammar in imitation, comprehension, and production. *J. verb. Learn. verb. Behav.,* 1963, **2**, 121-135.

Gvozdev, A. N. *Voprosy izucheniia detskoi rechi* (Problems in the language development of the child). Moscow: Academy of Pedagogical Science, 1961.

Miller, W., and Ervin, S. The development of grammar in child language. In U. Bellugi and R. Brown (Editors), The acquisition of language. *Child Developm. Monogr.*, 1964, **29**, 9-34.

Weir, R. H. *Language in the crib*. The Hague: Mouton, 1962.

Index

191

19

THE M.I.T. PRESS PAPERBACK SERIES